CAREER SEARCH

BY
SHERRY STRONG

COPYRIGHT © 1998 Mark Twain Media, Inc.
ISBN 1-58037-033-0
Printing No. CD–1306

Mark Twain Media, Inc., Publishers
Distributed by Carson-Dellosa Publishing Company, Inc.

The purchase of this book entitles the buyer to reproduce the student pages for classroom use only. Other permissions may be obtained by writing Mark Twain Media, Inc., Publishers.

All rights reserved. Printed in the United States of America.

TABLE OF CONTENTS

INTRODUCTION 1

CHAPTER 1: Would You Recognize a Career if It Bit You on the Leg? 2

CHAPTER 2: Careers Make the World Go 'Round 8

CHAPTER 3: Happiness is a Six-Letter Word 13

CHAPTER 4: What's Money Got to Do With It? 17

CHAPTER 5: You Can't Be a Dragon Slayer Forever 22

CHAPTER 6: You are Unique, and That is Good 28

CHAPTER 7: What Do You Think About You? 33

CHAPTER 8: What Makes You Tick? 39

CHAPTER 9: Testing. Testing. 1 . . . 2 . . . 3 47

CHAPTER 10: Polly Wants a Cracker 53

CHAPTER 11: Healthy or Toxic; Positive or Negative: The Choice is Yours 58

CHAPTER 12: Do You Know Where You are Going? 62

CHAPTER 13: Increasing Your Chances for Success 66

CHAPTER 14: Classroom Activities 71

CHAPTER 15: Tips for the Teacher 73

WHAT DO YOU THINK?: Self-Assessment 75

JUST BECAUSE OF YOU 77

BIBLIOGRAPHY 78

INTRODUCTION

"Blessed is he who has found his work; let him ask no other blessedness."

—Thomas Carlyle

This activity book is designed to encourage the student to take the first step into the world of careers. It is designed to help the student understand that a career is less a choice that has to be made and more an outlet for a student's unique talents and abilities.

This book is designed to encourage the student to get acquainted with his or her self and to understand the freedom and responsibility of choices when it comes to careers. Our efforts are directed at empowering the student to make effective career choices along the career development journey.

This book is designed to acquaint the student with processes and resources, with self-concept and self-awareness, with healthy and toxic choices, with responsibility and the effect of it all on career choice. This book offers room for the student to explore his or her self. It facilitates for the student the understanding that career choice is ultimately a matching of one's values, goals, purpose, and passion to the career that will allow the manifestation of those values, goals, purpose, and passion.

—The Author

CHAPTER 1
WOULD YOU RECOGNIZE A CAREER IF IT BIT YOU ON THE LEG?

Have you ever heard mothers or fathers talk about their child's future career? Even when a baby is just days old, a mother will sometimes remark, "Just look at my baby's long fingers! I think we have a future pianist in the family." Or maybe the father will proudly say, "Look at the size of my son, will you? Surely he is going to grow up to be a football linebacker."

While the child with the long fingers may never desire to play the piano, nor the large boy have an interest in football, parents who make such statements about their babies have the best intentions. They know the child will someday become an adult and will be a happier adult if he or she has found a satisfying life's work.

Have you ever thought about what you want to be when you are an adult? Just as parents realize that you will not be a child forever, you surely know that you will not be in middle school forever. Someday, in a few short years, you will be out of school, working at a job or career . . . unless you have a fairy godmother who zaps you with her magic wand and proclaims you king or queen of a kingdom.

Now you know that there is not much chance of a fairy godmother choosing your career for you. But, if you did get zapped by a fairy godmother and found yourself reigning over an empire, you had better have an excellent education and outstanding communication, accounting, computer, and managerial skills. So you see, even a monarch's career, though unique, requires much preparation.

Are you prepared to make a decision about the kind of career you want when you are grown? Probably not right now, but it is never too early to begin thinking about your abilities, your success, and the kind of work that you would someday like to do.

Before you get too anxious about choosing the career that is right for you, you need to address some very basic questions that will help you understand the world of careers. Before you finish this book, you will have a working knowledge of career choices. You will understand the nature of a career. You will know where to get assistance and additional information regarding careers. You will know when to take certain steps in your career journey, and you will learn why it is important for you to think about careers, to explore and learn about the world of careers, and to move along in your career development. You will understand that your career development is as important to your overall development as learning math, science, reading, and writing.

Before you can begin thinking about pursuing a career, shouldn't you know how to recognize a career when you see one? In order to recognize something, you have to know what it is. Right? Would you recognize a career if it bit you on the leg?

Think for a moment. . . . What if you had never heard of ice cream and had never tasted it. Even if you saw ice cream, having never heard about it, you probably would not recognize it.

The same goes for careers. If you do not know about careers and if you do not hear about the world of careers, then you might miss out on all the wonderful and exciting opportunities the world of careers offers you. You do not want to miss out on fulfilling your dreams, do you? Of course you don't.

Imagine for a moment that you have the following talents and skills: You think fast. You have a creative mind. You enjoy reading and are well-read. You love science and like to learn. You have great finger dexterity, that is, you can quickly manipulate objects with your fingers. You have a very good memory. You care about people and their well-being.

All these talents and skills can be applied to a number of professions or careers such as physician, computer scientist, astronaut, engineer, architect, journalist, college professor, surgeon, archeologist, clothing designer, chef, or even ichthyologist. Ichthyologist! What is an ichthyologist? If you have what it takes to be an ichthyologist, you might miss the opportunity to use your talents and abilities if you did not know that an ichthyologist is a biologist who studies fish.

Today the word *career* includes business, profession, vocation, purpose, or calling. This means that the word *career* has a very broad meaning. A **career** is the use of one's talents and abilities that are committed and used over one's lifetime, devoted to a purpose, a meaning, or lifelong goal, and are manifested or made known through work. Putting it simply, a career is one's lifelong work that is developed through training, education, and experience.

A **career field** or cluster is a grouping of related careers. For example there are many careers in the field or cluster of medicine and health. According to the *Dictionary of Occupational Titles,* which is published by the U. S. Government, some of the careers in the field of medicine and health are physicians and surgeons, osteopaths, dentists, veterinarians, pharmacists, registered nurses, therapists, dietitians, and occupations in medical and dental technology.

One can consider a career field as an umbrella. Under the umbrella of art, a number of careers could be listed—careers such as commercial art, design, illustration, graphic art, photography, painting, pottery, and sculpting.

A profession is a career, business, vocation, calling, or purpose. To say "within a profession" is referring to a group of related careers. Psychiatric nursing falls under the umbrella of nursing, which falls under the umbrella of medicine and health. Teaching falls under the umbrella of education. Preschool teaching falls under the umbrella of teaching.

Why not take a moment here and reread the definition of a career?

Where did we get the word *career?* In the French language, *une carriere* means "a career." *Carriere* is modified from the Latin word, *carraria,* or a "road for vehicles." The Latin word *carraria* comes from the Latin word, *carras,* meaning "wheeled vehicle." You might say that the word *career* can be translated as, "moving along a road." Actually, the word *career* does mean moving along a certain course.

If we apply these interpretations of the word *career,* we can assume that a career is a road that leads to someplace or somewhere. This is true with one's career choice. When you set out on a career path, there are always adventures along the "road" of career development. **Career development** is a progressive journey along the road to your ultimate career choice.

It is good to keep in mind that some career roads are easy and smooth, but some are difficult. Some career roads are very exciting, and some are less exciting. However, everyone's career road or path is significant or important.

When you see or visit someone in a career that you recognize, you do not see the time, the energy, and the effort that the individual had to put forth in order to achieve career success. You do not see the rough career roads that an individual had to "travel" in order to arrive at their present position.

When you visit your doctor, you might see your physician wearing a clean, white coat and you might see a stethoscope hanging around the doctor's neck. Your physician is competent, caring, and professional. But, what you do not see is what the doctor had to give up in order to learn about everything that relates to his or her career as a physician, everything from the use of a stethoscope and how it aides in detecting heart problems to communication with patients like you. Physicians must study long and hard and train for many years before earning the right to be called "doctor." Most likely, the doctor had limited time for fun and pleasure while learning and training.

Those who arrive at their destination and enjoy career satisfaction have traveled a rigorous road prior to arrival.

If you have ever used a road map in your travels, you know that in order to arrive at your destination, you must not only locate on the map where you will begin the journey, but you must also make the trip. While this sounds silly, it is a simple truth. To arrive at a certain place, you have to not only prepare for the trip, but you must also begin it, enjoy the pleasures it brings, and work through the difficulties it presents. Only then can you appreciate the journey.

With a career choice, it is the same. To enter into any career, you must find a guide or guides that will instruct you on the best way to achieve that career. You must know what you want to achieve or what career you want to pursue, and you must choose your own direction.

You have to prepare for career choice by developing your talents, abilities, and aptitudes and by acquiring information. Your attitude must help you to enjoy the benefits and pleasures while you work through the difficulties of your career development.

Remember that even a journey with a map in hand can present road blocks and detours. So it is with a career. But, much of the fun of a journey is getting there. Embarking upon a career road is one of the most exciting, demanding, yet satisfying roads of your life. The excitement comes from knowing that it is your "vehicle"—your career . . . and you are in the "driver's seat." By getting the proper training (**career guidance**), gaining adequate knowledge and information (**career maturity**), and taking the right steps (**career development**), you can set out on a most exciting and enlightening journey towards your career choice. Taking the proper career development steps will ensure that your career choice is the right one for you.

Career Search　　　　CHAPTER 1: Would You Recognize a Career if It Bit You on the Leg?

Name _____ Date _____

WHAT DO YOU THINK?

1. Did you ever hear someone remark about what career you might consider as an adult? If so, tell which career and why.

_____
_____
_____

2. Have you ever thought that you should consider a certain career for a particular reason? If so, name the career and explain why.

_____
_____
_____

3. Name three careers you have thought would be right for you as an adult. Explain why you have thought about them.

_____
_____
_____
_____

4. If you had a fairy godmother, what career do you think she would choose for you and why?

_____
_____
_____

5. Teaching is a career cluster. Can you think of at least five careers that would fall under the career cluster of teaching?

_____
_____
_____
_____
_____

© Mark Twain Media, Inc., Publishers

Career Search   CHAPTER 1: Would You Recognize a Career if It Bit You on the Leg?

Name _____ Date _____

6. What do the careers *veterinarian, nurse, pediatrician, physician's assistant,* and *orthopedic surgeon* have in common? Explain, as best you can, each of these careers.

_____
_____
_____
_____

7. On your way to school, you might see a police officer patrolling the streets, a store manager unlocking the doors of a store, or a truck driver headed out onto the highway. List some of the careers that you recognize as you come and go from school.

_____
_____
_____
_____

8. If *career* is defined as a purpose, or calling, or one life's work, what do you think would be the "calling" of a priest, minister, or rabbi?

_____
_____

9. What do you think would be the "purpose" of a gardener?

_____
_____

10. What would be the "life's work" of a piano teacher?

_____
_____

11. How would you define the "life's work" of a jeweler?

_____
_____

12. A professional ice skater's job is to make ice skating look easy. What do you think would be some of the rough "roads" of an ice skater's career?

_____
_____
_____

Career Search   CHAPTER 1: Would You Recognize a Career if It Bit You on the Leg?

Name _____ Date _____

13. What would be some of the benefits or rewards of becoming a doctor?

_____
_____
_____
_____

14. If you could choose any career in the world, what career would it be?

_____
_____

15. Now, explain what you would have to do in order to achieve that career.

_____
_____
_____
_____

16. What would be some of the more difficult tasks of achieving this career?

_____
_____
_____
_____

17. What would be some of the benefits or rewards of this career?

_____
_____
_____
_____

CHAPTER 2
CAREERS MAKE THE WORLD GO 'ROUND

Have you ever heard the saying, particularly around Valentine's Day, that "Love makes the world go 'round."? While we can agree or disagree that love does, indeed, make the world go 'round, let us consider something else that makes the world go 'round. Let us consider how careers make the world go 'round.

Consider all the careers and the people in them that make our world function, or "go 'round" each and every day. Motherhood is the career for rearing children. Teaching is the career for providing children with what they need to learn. Scientists research to find medicines and to understand diseases for prevention and cures for the world's people. Doctors and nurses help keep people well. Entertainers amuse and enlighten. Travel agents help us get to destinations around the globe. Engineers design and develop small and large products, from watches to bridges, from computer chips to enormous building structures. Electricians help power our homes and businesses. Counselors advise. Professors open doors of knowledge. Stylists and decorators beautify. Navigators help us stay on course. Sales people broaden our choices. Mechanics help keep us going. Chefs delight our tastes. Police officers increase our safety. Pilots expedite our journey. Therapists and clergy contribute to our understanding of life.

Yes . . . careers exist for the betterment of you, your family, and society in general. The quality of our lives and our world is dependent upon people in thousands of different careers. That is why all careers are important to the world, to nations, states, cities, schools, churches, and families.

Imagine for a moment if this world had no teachers. Okay, you might enjoy not going to school for a little while, but without a teacher, you would have to depend upon your family or friends to teach you everything—from reading to math, from physical education to art.

If the world had no farmers, who would produce our meat, milk, chicken, fruit, or vegetables? If the world had no scientists, who would find ways to eradicate pollution, hunger, and disease? Indeed, we need careers in which people can make this world a better place to live.

As we grow older, careers become a part of our adult identity. One's characteristics, talents, abilities, and attitudes are all part of the person who enters a career. The career becomes the vehicle or the host for the person to use those talents and abilities. Therefore, it is only natural that we sometimes identify a person by his or her career, for it is through the career that the individual has expressed his or her self.

When you think of Abraham Lincoln, do you immediately think of him as President Lincoln and what he accomplished in his presidency?

We identify President Lincoln by his career. If you were to write a biography on just about anyone, you would most likely consider his or her accomplishments achieved through his or her career. A professional athlete's career is the vehicle that enables the athlete to express talent. An astronaut's career is the vehicle that enables the astronaut to express an aptitude for science. A career as a mother is the vehicle that enables the mother to express her talents and abilities to rear children.

Many times when an adult is first introduced to another, one of the first questions asked is, "What do you do?". This question is a way of getting better acquainted. It is asked early in a conversation simply because careers are important in our daily lives. Moreover, when an adult asks another adult, "What do you do?", it is another way of saying, I want to know you better; I want to relate to you better. If you tell me about the kind of work you do, I can understand you better. I can relate to work because I work or I have worked in the past.

Careers help define who we are, who we communicate with, and who we work with. Careers help determine who we turn to for help and who we turn to for education, health, and recreation. The world focuses on careers because they play an integral or important role in the well-being and meaning of our lives and our future.

Careers play a role even in the lives of preschoolers. Have you ever observed a preschool or a room full of preschool age children? Notice when preschoolers are exposed to a play environment complete with toy kitchens, doctor kits, toy pianos, art brushes and paint, dolls and carriages, construction toys, firefighter hats, or even something as simple as a piece of chalk, these very young children have the creativity and imagination to become a homemaker, doctor, nurse, pianist, artist, child care worker, engineer, architect, firefighter, or teacher.

Give a preschooler a hairbrush, and you have a mini-hairstylist. Give the child a toy microphone, and you have a singer. Give a child a toy dog, and you have a very young veterinarian or dog groomer. Children, as early as age two or three, learn and know some very basic career information. For a few minutes in a play period, a child can choose to be anything from a gardener to a musician. For a few playtime minutes, they are no longer just a preschooler, they are royalty or a scientist, a dancer or a chef. But tomorrow they may choose to be something else.

After observing preschool play for a short time, you may discover that children frequently go from one pretend career role to another. For a few minutes, little Jane may pretend that she is an astronaut, but it won't be long before she is in another area of the room pretending, with the help of building blocks, that she is an engineer. After tiring of engineering, little Jane may have enough time today to visit another play station and pretend that she is a teacher.

Preschoolers have the luxury of pretending without the responsibility of actually learning, in depth, about the career. A preschooler is not aware that an architect must have a degree in architecture and a lot of training, or that an astronaut must have an extensive education in science and be able to withstand much physical stress. Therefore, a preschooler can play out many career roles with no worries about the actual requirements of a career.

Adults cannot change careers every 15 minutes like preschoolers, but adults do change jobs, from five to seven times during their adult lives. The reasons for change may vary, but change within a career cluster is not unusual. In fact, it is very normal. Some nurses have gone on to medical school, which is staying within the career of medicine. Some police officers become private detectives, which is a move within the criminal justice system. Some horticulturists (an expert in growing and caring for plants) open their own greenhouses or shops where they sell what they grow. That is staying within the career of horticulture but entering into the profession of retail, as well.

Many adults change from one career field or cluster to another. People have left teaching for nursing, coaching for broadcasting, selling for counseling, piloting for teaching, managing for litigating (or working as a courtroom lawyer), or researching for a career in medicine. When an adult moves from one particular career, sometimes the reason is not unlike the reason a preschooler changes a career—because the adult is bored and wants something different or new. Sometimes a change comes because an adult may realize a new potential or talent within themselves, and they want to put that talent or ability to use in a new career. Or, advances in technology may force one out of a career. Years ago, elevators had elevator operators. Years ago, if you wanted to make a telephone call, you had to do it through a telephone operator. Today those jobs are no longer in existence due to advances in technology.

With people making career changes, it is possible that your dentist may have had a totally different career before a career in dentistry. Perhaps your coach may have once been a salesperson, or a police officer in your community may have once been a karate teacher. Maybe your teacher had another career prior to teaching at your school.

People change careers for many reasons, and most often, the change is good for them and for the world. With any career change, a person can take his or her present talent, ability, and knowledge and transfer it to another career. Of course, the nurse who goes on to medical school to become a doctor can certainly use any knowledge acquired as a nurse. But even a change outside of a career—an attorney who becomes a fiction writer or an accountant who becomes a homemaker and mother—still allows one to use the knowledge and expertise of one career in a new career. The attorney can apply the knowledge of law to understand laws relating to a writing career, such as copyright law. The accountant can apply the knowledge of accounting to effective financial planning for the family.

The world goes 'round with the help of creative, talented, and dedicated people who apply their talents and abilities to the betterment of the world. When you see people performing their work, think about how the work they are doing contributes to making the world a better place for you. Then, think about how you can make the world a better place . . . and you have probably found a good clue about a career path for yourself. Wouldn't you like to help make the world go 'round? Of course you would. The world needs you and your talents and abilities.

Career Search CHAPTER 2: Careers Make the World Go 'Round

Name _____ Date _____

WHAT DO YOU THINK?

1. Explain how you think careers help make the world go 'round.

_____
_____
_____
_____

2. Name two careers and explain how these careers help make the world a better place to live.

_____
_____
_____

3. How would your life be different if the world had no artists?

_____
_____
_____

4. Name three adults you know, and identify their careers.

_____
_____
_____

5. Name three adults you know who have changed careers.

_____
_____
_____

6. What career roles do you remember playing as a young child?

_____
_____
_____

© Mark Twain Media, Inc., Publishers

Name _____ Date _____

7. Which career role did you think was the most fun to play when you were very young? Why?

_____

_____

_____

_____

8. Explain how a speech writer and a singer could help the world.

_____

_____

_____

_____

9. If you chose to be a cartoonist, how could you make the world a better place in which to live?

_____

_____

_____

_____

10. Name three skills that a nurse might transfer to a career as a school teacher.

_____

_____

_____

_____

11. Name three skills that a school teacher might transfer to a career as a police officer.

_____

_____

_____

_____

CHAPTER 3
HAPPINESS IS A SIX-LETTER WORD

Some people do not think of their careers as work. These people go to their businesses or offices or studios or wherever they perform their work because they "love it." They love their work. They love doing what they do best. They love putting their unique talents and abilities to work. They love expressing themselves through their careers.

People who love what they do do not always refer to their careers as work; they view their careers as vehicles that carry their talents and abilities closer toward their goal or purpose.

A **goal** is an objective or what one wants to achieve. A **purpose** is the reason one wants to achieve a goal. A purpose is why one gets up in the morning or why one goes to work.

There are some people who actually perform their work in their careers without monetary reward or money. No kidding! An example of working without pay would be homemakers and mothers who do not, usually, receive a paycheck or money for what they do.

Confucius, a Chinese philosopher who lived from 551 to 478 B.C., once said, "Choose a job you love, and you will never have to work a day in your life."

People who love what they do, who enjoy performing their career's work, are generally very happy people. Some people will say that they are happy in their career because they have found their "calling" or they are serving their purpose. In other words, the work that they do, want to do, and need to do matches the work that the career requires. This match of the person with the work helps to make the person content, satisfied, or happy. An individual can perform in a chosen career the kind of work that he or she truly enjoys doing. In other words, a person can express him or herself in a chosen career.

Knowing about careers and all that one must do to enter a career is important. But why is it important? Why are there so many books written about career planning and development, about the kinds of careers in the world today, and about how to choose a career? And why is it important that you learn about yourself, your interests, and the kinds of careers that interest you? So that you will grow into a satisfied, contented, happy adult.

The reason you learn and progress through career development or objective planning related to careers is that when you become an adult, you will be doing the kind of work that makes you happy. When, as an adult, you can see and feel that the work you do is directly related to your goal or purpose, you will not only feel a sense of happiness, you will feel a sense of overall contentment and accomplishment, a feeling that you are "on track" and doing what you were intended to do. When you know that you are using your talents and abilities in your work, you will be much happier than if you are not.

Have you ever been asked, "What are you going to be when you grow up?" When you are asked that question by a well-meaning adult, the adult does not expect you to choose a career right now. What they are conveying to you is that they believe in you. They believe you will be a success. They believe that you will choose a career that will use your talents and abilities. Most importantly, they believe you will grow up to be a happy adult. They WANT you to become a happy adult.

Does a career make a person happy? It helps. Research has shown that if people use their unique talents and abilities or express their unique selves in their daily work, they will be happier than if they do not. Studies show that matching one's talents and abilities with a career that utilizes or uses those talents and abilities gives one a greater chance of satisfaction and happiness.

What are talents? What are abilities? You are born with **talents** and **aptitudes**. You acquire or learn skills and abilities. A talent or aptitude is like a tool that must be used, a tool that you cannot put down or set aside. If you are in a career in which the tool you possess cannot be used, experts believe that you could become discontented, frustrated, or even depressed.

An **ability** or **skill** is something you acquire, like reading, writing, skateboarding, or swimming. However, keep in mind that some people are born with a talent for these things and can acquire the skill very quickly. Think of people who have beautiful penmanship or of Olympic swimmers. Many people can acquire a skill, but not everyone has the same talent.

Years ago a man by the name of Johnson O'Connor felt very strongly about helping others find success. Mr. O'Connor came to believe and understand that people are happiest when they are in the kind of work where they can use their unique talents or aptitudes. Today the Johnson O'Connor Research Foundation, Inc., has offices in major cities throughout the country. The Foundation continues to provide clients, through testing, with valuable information about their aptitudes, which when applied to careers, can lead to individual success and happiness.

Try to imagine two women—Jill and Jane. Jill is tired of her work. She gets up every morning and wishes that she did not have to go in. But, it is a job, and she needs the money. This wasn't the kind of job Jill had imagined herself doing. She had given up on her career dream years ago. It wasn't her fault. Things just happened that way. So, she took a job just to earn a living. At work, Jill does only what she has to do and nothing more. Much of the time she finds herself watching the clock, waiting for the work day to end. She realizes that her best days at work are the days that she gets paid.

Jane loves her work. She gets up every morning and looks forward to getting to work. She is very good at her work. In fact, she got the job in the first place because she always had an interest in this kind of work. Even as a teenager, Jane thought she might like to do some kind of work that related to this career. "What a lucky person I am," Jane thinks to herself as she drives to work. The morning goes by swiftly for Jane. Before she knows it, it is lunch time. After that, the day flies by. There just doesn't seem to be enough time to do all she'd like to do. But, Jane concludes, there is always another day. And she looks forward to tackling this when she gets back to work tomorrow. One day Jane told one of her friends, "I like this work so much, I can't believe that I get paid for doing something that I love."

Yes, career information plays a key role in your happiness as an adult. So dive in, explore, examine, and learn all that you can. There is a career waiting just for you. So get ready, get set, and go after it. Your happiness could depend upon it.

Career Search CHAPTER 3: Happiness is a Six-Letter Word

Name _____ Date _____

WHAT DO YOU THINK?

1. Think of an adult whom you think is happy in his or her work. Name the adult and tell what work he or she does.
_____
_____
_____

2. If a career is for self-expression, a way to achieve a purpose through the use of one's talents and abilities, what talents do you think a dog trainer would possess?
_____
_____
_____

3. What, do you think, are the talents and abilities of your school teacher?
_____
_____
_____

4. What do you think the Chinese philosopher, Confucius, meant by, "Choose a job you love, and you will never have to work a day in your life."?
_____
_____
_____
_____

5. What kind of work, activity, or hobby makes you happy when you do it? How did you become interested in this work, activity, or hobby?
_____
_____
_____

6. If, as an adult, you could make the world a better place in which to live, what career would you choose?
_____
_____

© Mark Twain Media, Inc., Publishers

Career Search   CHAPTER 3: Happiness is a Six-Letter Word

Name _____ Date _____

7. What talents or aptitudes do you have that would make the world a better place?
_____
_____
_____
_____

8. What things are you learning in school that, as an adult, you can use to make the world a better place?
_____
_____
_____
_____

9. Are there any abilities or skills you particularly want to acquire before you graduate from high school? What are they, and why are they important to you?
_____
_____
_____
_____

10. Do you have a "purpose" or a "calling"? How would you define your "purpose"?
_____
_____
_____
_____

11. What can you do today to increase your chances for happiness within a career as an adult?
_____
_____
_____
_____

CHAPTER 4
WHAT'S MONEY GOT TO DO WITH IT?

Experts agree that finding a career in which you can use your talents and abilities can lead to personal satisfaction, contentment, and happiness. So, naturally, you might think that the only reason you pursue a career is so you can "be happy." That is a nice, simple cause and effect—career and happiness, but "happiness" is not the only reason for a satisfying career.

Aristotle, a Greek philosopher who lived from 384 to 322 B.C., was quoted as having said, "First, have a definite, clear, practical ideal—a goal, an objective. Second, have the necessary means to achieve your ends—wisdom, money, materials, and methods. Third, adjust all your means to that end."

What did Aristotle mean by "have the necessary means to achieve your ends"? He was saying that in order to achieve your goal, you must have what it takes. He was saying that you must have what it takes to win. What this means is, to be a "top" anything, to be a "winner," you must have what it takes. To be a top athlete, you must have what it takes. To be an "A" student, you must have what it takes. To learn to drive a car, you must have what it takes. To succeed at anything, you must have what it takes.

Can Aristotle's rule apply to having the comforts you want out of life? Absolutely. To have the comforts of life, you must have what it takes. And what does it take to have the comforts of life? Most often, money. And to get money, you must earn it. To earn money, you must have what is referred to as **earning power**.

What is earning power? Earning power is the ability to earn money. The extent or the range of how much and how fast you earn your money is your earning power. To have earning power, you must have what it takes . . . which is a career, a business, a profession—whatever it takes.

Unless your hope is to win the lottery or inherit enormous wealth or call upon that imaginary fairy godmother, you are better off with developing your earning power through a career. All careers give you earning power. However, there are careers where you might expect to earn more money than in other careers where you should expect to earn less. The amount of earning power within each career field is dependent upon, most often, the economy and one's education and training.

When the economy is strong or healthy, people have jobs and people use the money they earn from those jobs to invest in the nation's goods and services. With a strong economy, your chances of entering the career of your choice are greater simply because there are more jobs, so more people get hired.

A second factor in career earning power is the amount of education and training required for a career. Usually, the more education and/or training required, the higher the earning power or the more money earned. Studies have shown that, on the average, a college degree will bring a higher salary than a high school diploma. An advanced degree will bring a higher salary than a bachelor's degree. A doctor's degree will bring a higher salary than a master's degree.

A physical therapist is someone who prescribes a course of therapy to help people rehabilitate—recover or improve from an illness, injury, or disability. A physical therapist, sometimes referred to as a "PT," has the potential for high earning power. Why? Because a physical therapist must earn an undergraduate college degree, an advanced or master's degree, and must undergo many hours of hands-on training and observation. Earning the title of "physical therapist" takes years of effort and a commitment of time and energy, as well as a great deal of money to pay for the education.

A child-care worker, someone who cares for children in their home or in a child-care facility, has less earning power than a physical therapist. Does that mean that a career as a physical therapist is more important than a career as a child-care worker? Absolutely not. Remember, some people are happier in an environment where they can use their talents and abilities as a physical therapist and some people are happier in the child-care environment. However, because a career in physical therapy requires many more years of education and training and more money for education, the earning power of a physical therapist is stronger than that of a child-care worker. Usually, a child-care worker is not required to have a college degree but is often required to have some amount of training.

Does this mean that everyone with a college education has more earning power than someone without a college education? No. There are people who have become very wealthy by virtue of creating or inventing something. Writers are a good example. If an author writes a book that becomes very popular, that author can earn a lot of money whether he or she has a college education or not. However, going to college helps people learn to write better. Therefore, learning more usually means earning more.

Let us consider what earning power or the power to earn money can mean to your future. First of all, it is important to note that money, in and of itself, is just money. Let's say that you had a career and you earned money. Each time you got paid, you put that money in a big box under your bed. Each year, you would open the box and count all your money. You just liked looking at your money. You never spent it; you just counted it.

Because you never spent your money on anything, your clothes began to look old and ragged, your car quit running because you failed to maintain it, and your house had no heating, air conditioning, water, or electricity because you did not want to spend money. By the time you got to this point of no water, electricity, or food, your life had become pretty sad. But, you had lots and lots of money under your bed.

Does having a lot of money mean that you have a wonderful life? No. Having a lot of money that is used wisely means that you could have a quality, comfortable life. Money is a tool that is used to get the things you need and want.

Obviously, the more money you have, the more tools you can have to surround yourself with the kind of life that is important to you.

With money being the tool or the product of your earning power, let us look at money and what it means. What if there were a 20 dollar ($20) bill hidden between the pages of this book. Would finding $20 be your earning power? No. Finding money is not earning money. However, if you found $20 in this book, you would have $20 worth of buying power. Earning power is different from buying power.

Earning power is, again, how fast and how much money one earns. **Buying power** or purchasing power is the amount of money or wealth one has with which to buy or purchase. Earning power relates to one's buying power. What you earn determines your buying power. How much and how fast you earn is your earning power. Money is what you earn, and the amount of money you have at a given time is your buying power.

So, if you found $20, you have that much money with which to buy something. Just like the word *career* is a word that means a lot of things to a lot of people, the word *money* means a lot of things to a lot of people. The word *money* is a powerful word. In fact, notice the terms used in association with money—earning *power* and buying *power*. Our society tends to associate money and power. While there is truth in the saying, "Money doesn't buy happiness," money can buy a comfortable life. *Comfortable* is a subjective word, or a word that means different things to different people. But, most people would agree that a comfortable life is living the kind of life and having the kind of lifestyle that you want.

Someone who lives on a farm, many miles away from the nearest residence, may be very happy. The farmer may consider getting up at 4:00 A.M. every morning to milk the cows a comfortable life. The farmer must earn enough money to buy cows and equipment to maintain the kind of life that the farmer wants. This is true for the stage entertainer who does not have to be at work until 5:00 P.M. but works until midnight. The entertainer must have costumes, makeup, transportation, as well as a place to live when traveling. The entertainer must have enough earning power to maintain the kind of life that the entertainer wants.

As an adult you have the opportunity to enter the career that would make you happy and provide you with the earning power or buying power that would enable you to live the kind of life and lifestyle you want. While money is not everything, money is the tool that allows you to purchase those things or the lifestyle that would make you happy.

Remember, money does not just buy you "things." It buys comforts like electricity, water, heat, and cooling. It buys protection from injury—protection such as smoke alarms, bicycle helmets, car safety seats for babies, and sunglasses for your eyes. Money also buys prevention and cures—vaccinations from the doctor for measles, mumps, chickenpox, and polio. Money buys cures for cuts, wounds, and broken bones and buys treatments for mental illnesses such as depression and schizophrenia.

Money buys the little things like a telephone call to your best friend who lives in a state or country far away. Money can buy you a pet dog and the preventive shots and nutrition to keep a dog healthy. Money can buy flowers for your mother, an apple for your teacher, postage for your letter, or an airline ticket to Bangkok or the "Big Apple." But remember those words in the song that The Beatles once sang, "Money can't buy me love."

Whatever your earning power, the money you earn is a tool you use to develop and create the quality of life you want to live. The career road you choose to take will enable you to arrive at your destination or the lifestyle of your dreams. So whether you choose a career as a nurse, teacher, biochemist, rancher, firefighter, restaurant manager, or hairstylist, your earning power starts with you. You have the opportunity to determine your earning power by your learning power.

Name _____ Date _____

WHAT DO YOU THINK?

1. What kinds of things do you need in life, as a middle school student, to be happy?
   _____
   _____
   _____

2. What kinds of things do you have now that you could do without and still be a happy person?
   _____
   _____
   _____

3. Describe the kind of life you would like to have when you become an adult.
   _____
   _____
   _____
   _____

4. What career would help you best achieve the life you describe?
   _____

5. What kind of career do you see yourself engaged in when you become an adult?
   _____

6. What kind of education will you need to enter into this career?
   _____
   _____

7. What kind of earning power do you think you would have in this kind of career?
   _____
   _____

8. What is the difference between earning power and buying power?
   _____
   _____
   _____

Name _____ Date _____

9. Do you think money can buy happiness? Why or why not?

_____
_____

10. If someone told you that the more time you put into school work and studying, the more earning and buying power you will have as an adult, what would you think? Would this, in any way, change the way you currently spend your time? Why or why not?

_____
_____
_____

11. Money can buy you an opportunity to earn a college degree. A college degree can earn you more earning and buying power as an adult. How does this information affect your career planning?

_____
_____
_____

12. If you had to choose between working in a career in which you were not happy, but made a lot of money, OR working in a career in which you were very happy, but made very little money, which would you choose? Explain your choice.

_____
_____
_____

13. List seven careers in which you think you would be happy as an adult.

_____
_____

Now, list the careers in the order of the least education or training to the most education or training required.

_____
_____

Now list the seven careers in the order of their earning power, from the least to the most.

_____
_____

CHAPTER 5
YOU CAN'T BE A DRAGON SLAYER FOREVER

Preschool and elementary school play time is sometimes spent on exploring roles. Pretending to be a play director, a minister, a pilot, and even a dragon slayer is a child's first step toward career awareness or career development. Pretending or role-playing demonstrates a child's knowledge about the world of purpose, opportunity, and work.

We know that as children get older, they turn away from pretending or role-playing to fact-finding about careers. Part of career development or objective career planning is giving up the pretending, "Hey, look at me!" stage and picking up the fact-finding mission. As a young child, you may have pretended to be a cosmetologist (one who studies cosmetics to beautify the face), but as you enter the fact-finding stage, you put real effort into finding out the work, education, and training that is required to become a cosmetologist rather than pretending to be one.

As a middle school student, you have made a transition or have moved from pretending to reality. You are ready to learn facts and more in-depth information about careers. This information will help you when you are ready to choose your career path.

When you were much younger, you may have pretended to be a teacher. At that time your idea of a teacher may have consisted of holding a pointer to a chalk board and telling your playmates what to do. Now you know, through observation, that there is more to being a teacher than just pointing at a chalkboard and telling children what to do.

You know, just from watching your own teacher, that a teacher has lesson plans to prepare, daily assignments to carry out, papers to grade, parent-teacher conferences to coordinate, meetings and conferences to attend, technology to learn and teach, and students to encourage and, yes, even to discipline. You know that your teacher must interact with the principal, the superintendent, parents, students, and other teachers. Your teacher must take part in lunchroom supervision, hallway monitoring, and extracurricular activities. Your teacher's job is to create the best learning environment for you, ensure that the material used is the best for you, and see that you are learning just as you should.

Preschoolers and elementary students do not comprehend all teacher-related duties, responsibilities, and rewards. And you, who probably once pretended to be the teacher with your playmates, have "graduated" from pretending to knowing.

Maybe when you were a small child, you made a homemade astronaut's helmet out of a plastic milk jug and pipe cleaners. Now, instead of pretending to be an astronaut, you can go to the library, get on the Internet, and watch programs about space and astronaut training. You can discover that astronauts must go to college, must undergo rigorous mental and physical testing, and must wear state-of-the-art space suits and much more sophisticated helmets than the one you may have, years ago, created. You, who may have once pretended to be an astronaut, have the opportunity now to really become one.

You can know that if your dream is to one day fly aboard a space shuttle and conduct experiments in space, you have within you the ability to make that happen. If your dream to fly into space is persistent, you can seek and receive help to make that dream a reality. For a moment, picture yourself in a state-of-the-art, twenty-first-century spacesuit, waving to the world via satellite, as you board the space shuttle. You know your mission. You have trained well. The countdown has begun. Isn't it exciting to discover that you no longer have to pretend? You can know that there is a career waiting out there for you—and the countdown has begun!

Moving from that time in your young life of role-playing in careers to learning factual information about careers is part of your **career development** or your progression and maturity in career planning and career awareness. According to experts in the field of career research, there are stages of career development, just as there are stages in physical and mental development.

As a baby, there were tasks you had to learn before you could "graduate" or move on to the next task. You had to learn to crawl before you could walk. You learned to make funny sounds like "goo goo" before you could talk. You were, at first, primarily interested in your own fingers and toes before you shifted your interest to other people.

All of us work through developmental stages, or different sets of objectives, that we must master in order to "graduate" to the next stage. We begin to go through these stages as soon as we are born and continue going through stages throughout life. Each stage that we successfully complete strengthens our foundation for life's opportunities and challenges.

After you learned the alphabet, you learned to read and write, preparing you for more opportunities and challenges. After you learned to walk and run, you learned to do things like ride a bicycle, glide on a skateboard, or rollerblade. Each task you master opens up new opportunities and challenges for you.

Knowing and understanding physical and mental developmental stages helps those who care for you know if you are progressing as you should. Guidelines for physical and mental developmental stages were formulated by doctors, researchers, and scientists and are part of a pediatrician's training. If a child has not achieved a particular developmental stage by a certain age, tests are taken to investigate why. Then measures are taken to assist the child in reaching the appropriate developmental stage.

Experts in the field of career study theorize that, like physical and mental development, there are a number of career developmental stages that everyone should pass through. A **developmental theory** is a method used to measure one's progress or lack of progress. A developmental theory helps you to know if you are in the appropriate career developmental stage for your age and your situation or circumstance.

We noted earlier that as you grow up, you leave the play and pretend world of career development. As a middle school student, you should have put away your early childhood toys and ways. To use the developmental stage theory as a method of measurement, let's ask you a question: What kinds of things do you like to do after school? If you answer, "I like to put a sack on top of my head, borrow my mom's apron, and use toy spoons to pretend that I am a chef," then you would know that you, a middle school student, are NOT in the appropriate career development stage.

However, if a career as a chef is interesting to you and your answer to the above question is something like, "I like to cook. I like to bake cookies for my friends," or "I like to collect recipes from magazines and create my own cookbook," then it is obvious that you are in the appropriate developmental stage. When you leave pretending for fact-finding and "trying on" careers, you have progressed in your career development.

Middle school is an exciting time of career development. This is because there is always something new to explore and something new to learn about careers and the world of careers and about yourself. While you are "window shopping," or just looking at all the world has to offer you in the way of a future and a career, you are also maturing in your acquisition and assimilation of career information. In other words, you are seeking, finding, and using the information you gather about careers.

This time of career development is a very busy and demanding time for you, but it is your "job" to learn about the world of careers and about yourself: your strengths, weaknesses, likes, and dislikes. These tasks of career development must be completed or mastered before you can move on to another stage of career development, which takes you even closer to making a career choice.

Part of the career development of middle school students involves career exploration via any media. This means that career discovery can be accomplished through virtually any source—textbooks in the classroom, speakers in and out of the classroom, videos, the library, the Internet, television, newspapers, mentors (someone you admire for their achievements and success), and more.

While you are gathering information, you are also trying that information "on for size." In other words, while you are learning about a specific career, you are often applying it directly to yourself. For example, while learning about a career as a dentist, you are not pretending you are a dentist; rather you are thinking and wondering if a career as a dentist "fits" or is appropriate for you.

You might attend science fairs to check your level of interest in the sciences. When you have an appointment with your own dentist, you might ask questions about the career of a dentist. You might ask the dentist what it was like to choose dentistry as a career. As you are "trying out" this idea of becoming a dentist, you are gathering more information, not only about the work and requirements of a dentist, but whether or not it is appealing to you. You may or may not see yourself studying science and attending college for many years before becoming a dentist.

This tentative process of career shopping and trying a career on for size is all part of your career development. And it is fun to do. You can shop all kinds of places and your choices are infinite. Be aware that while you are "career shopping," you are developing your own lists of likes and dislikes, your own preferences, desires, and values. This is the nature of your career development process and you are, now, in one of the developmental stages.

Once you have developed to a point of narrowing your focus, or choosing one or two career options, you have left one developmental stage for another; a stage that will see you through to actually entering your career choice.

Be aware that the career development period during the middle school years is not easy, for much of the decisions will be yours, unlike when you were a child and your caregivers instructed and guided your every move. As indicated before, the road to a career is not always smooth. Sometimes it is, but often it is not. The middle school years can be a rough road, but it has its smooth parts, as well. Keep in mind that while you have the gift of opportunity to look at and consider every career in existence, you are also experiencing change within and without yourself. That is, you are going through physical developmental stages, too.

Physical and mental development for a middle school student can be challenging, especially when career development is going on at the same time. Sometimes life can appear to be overwhelming, but remember that adults have "been there." They have experienced what you are experiencing, and they understand the difficulties development can present. Do not be shy about asking for time to talk with a trusted adult. Talking with an adult could help lighten your burdens, which may, at times, feel quite beyond your ability to carry. Talking with a trusted adult can mean the difference between achieving or not achieving your dreams.

A good question to ask here is, "Does everybody move through the career development process at the same time, in the same way?" The answer is no. When considering physical and developmental stages for babies and toddlers, we know that all babies do not begin to talk at the same time, cut teeth at the same time, or walk at the same time. Some develop early, some later, and some in between. Development, while everyone experiences it, is unique to the individual. So it is with career development.

Remember, career development is good, but just like physical, emotional, and mental development, it is something new and is sometimes confusing. It may help you to know that every one of your peers is going through the same thing you are, and it may be a challenging time for them as well. But ultimately, career development is the road to your dreams.

Career Search — CHAPTER 5: You Can't Be a Dragon Slayer Forever

Name _____ Date _____

WHAT DO YOU THINK?

1. Name three careers in which you have been interested for some time. Explain why you think these careers have appealed to you.

_____
_____
_____
_____

3. What could you do to find out more about a career as an orchestra conductor?

_____
_____
_____

4. What kinds of interests or hobbies do you think you would have if you had an interest in a career as an orchestra conductor?

_____
_____

5. Name seven careers about which you would like to know more.

_____
_____
_____

6. Name three adults and tell what kind of work they do.

_____
_____

Explain why you would or would not enjoy the work they do.

_____
_____
_____
_____

Career Search   CHAPTER 5: You Can't Be a Dragon Slayer Forever

Name _____ Date _____

7. How is your school helping you learn more about careers?
_____
_____
_____

8. What can you do on your own to learn more about the world of careers?
_____
_____
_____

9. Why is it important that you learn as much as possible about careers at this stage of your life?
_____
_____
_____

10. Name three adults who you think you could talk with about any changes you may be experiencing in your life. Explain why you think these adults would be helpful to you.
_____
_____
_____

11. Name your three favorite television programs and explain why these are your favorites.
_____
_____
_____

12. Are there any careers that you can identify in these programs? List them.
_____
_____

13. Do have any interest in any of the careers that are represented in your favorite television programs?
_____
_____

© Mark Twain Media, Inc., Publishers

CHAPTER 6
YOU ARE UNIQUE, AND THAT IS GOOD

A sperm cell and an egg cell unite and produce a cell containing 23 pairs of chromosomes. That cell divides into two cells, and those two cells unite. Then those cells divide and unite. Eventually, after all these cells divide and come together, a baby, made up of billions of cells, is formed.

Within these cells that form a baby are chromosomes. Within these chromosomes are genes. Within the genes is what is called DNA. DNA, or deoxyribonucleic acid, is what determines what we inherit from our birth parents and our ancestors. Those inherited characteristics, such as hair and eye color, height, and skin color, play a role in what makes one an individual or a unique person, different from any other human being on this earth.

The environment, like heredity, also plays a role in a person's growth and development. The environment, generally speaking, is anything that has an effect or influence on one's life. Like heredity, the environment plays a role in what makes a person unique or different.

Some experts argue that heredity has more effect on making the individual who he or she is than the environment. They argue that the DNA of your parents carries more of an impact on your life than anything else.

On the other hand, other experts argue that even a cell has its own unique environment, therefore environment at least equals the impact of heredity. However, experts continue to debate over the amount to which environment affects a baby's life after its birth. Whichever—heredity versus environment—they both have played a dramatic part in making up who you are, from the color of your eyes to the kind of music you enjoy.

Let's say that John inherited green eyes and black skin. He lives with his sister and parents on a dairy farm. He has learned to play the violin very well. Bill inherited brown eyes and white skin. He likes sports and plays on his school's soccer team. He lives with his three brothers, mother, and grandmother in a house near the mall in a large city. John and Bill are different from one another and are unique in comparison. Everyone is unique or different from another as a result of heredity and environment.

Just as people are unique in their appearance and personality, everyone is unique in talent and ability. If this were not the case, everyone would look the same, talk the same, and want to end up in the same career. If it were not for the wonder of uniqueness and differences, we would not have the wide variety of careers available today that we do.

If it were not for the wonder of differences in individuals, we would not have artists, engineers, scientists, teachers, horticulturists, equestrians, entertainers, journalists, politicians, or athletes—for we would be the same, not different. Moreover, we would not have the products of these careers. We would be without art, bridges, cures for diseases, food, and all the inventions that various careers produce.

Just imagine for a moment that everyone was a star basketball player. That would be amusing for a while. But, if everyone were a basketball player, there would be no carpenters, nurses, poets, and no other career for you to consider. It would be a boring world, indeed, if everyone were alike, if there were no differences among people.

Like all people, you have your own unique talent and special innate ability. Talents or aptitudes are inherited, just like your eye, skin, and hair color are inherited. Your talent or aptitude is part of what makes you unique.

There lies within you a talent, an aptitude, something that you can develop if you work at it. You have a talent that helps you do something a little better, maybe even a lot better than others. You may have learned to shoot baskets better than others. Perhaps you can run faster than most. Are you exceptionally good at math? Science? Art? Do you sing well? Play the flute? Are you good at story telling? Do you have a special ability to talk with people and make them feel at ease? Maybe you have developed a mature sense of business by having a paper route or by walking dogs in your neighborhood. Whatever your unique ability or talent, pay attention to it, take care to develop it, and put effort into perfecting it.

A special talent is what makes you unique or different. That uniqueness helps create choices and variety in your life and in the lives of others. The talent of a professional basketball player gives you the opportunity to watch an exciting ball game. The talent of an artist allows you to see the world from a different perspective. The talent of a nurse allows you to recover faster from an illness or injury.

Imagine the waste of talent if Mark Twain or Will Rogers had never written. What would the world be like today if Ludwig van Beethoven had not composed music or performed? What if Thomas Edison had not perfected his talent of inventing, or if Albert Einstein had set aside his interest in math? What if Martin Luther King had not preached? Imagine the world today without the impact of Margaret Mead, Helen Keller, Emily Dickinson, Mahatma Ghandi, Sojourner Truth, Maria Tallchief, or George Washington Carver. Imagine the world void of *your* talents.

If any of the names mentioned here are unfamiliar to you, you would benefit by dashing to your library to read about these people and their talents, which benefitted and changed the world.

To recognize your own talents or aptitudes, you need **self-knowledge**, or knowledge about yourself. You cannot begin to select the right career for yourself if you do not know your special talents.

Studies have indicated that it is actually easier to know someone else than it is to know yourself. Knowing one's self is not as easy as it sounds because it is easy to look at positive traits and not so easy to look at or face one's negative traits.

If someone said to you, "Tell me about a member of your family," you could probably describe many positive or good traits about this family member. After you mentioned many good things, you would probably be tempted to add a few not-so-good things. You might say that the family member you are describing dresses neatly, finishes homework, and is polite to others. Because you have known this person for a good while, you could even comment on some of his or her bad habits. You might say that the family member eats too much junk food, does not return borrowed items, and sometimes is too bossy. Yes, it is much easier to see the negative traits in others than in yourself. But, in order to really know you as you should, you must know the negative as well as the positive.

If you know and accept just the positive things about yourself and ignore and deny the negative things about yourself, aren't you accepting just a part of you? Why tell yourself, "I will accept and understand the wonderful, positive part of me, but I'm not interested in the rest of me, the part that is undesirable or not so wonderful"?

To be the successful adult that you will someday become, you must accept all that is you—the negative as well as the positive, because the negative is still you. Does this mean that you should just accept the negative things and do nothing about them? No.

The reason it is important to recognize and know the negative things about yourself is so these things will not ruin your chances for a happy life and successful career. If negative traits and habits go unchecked or unrecognized, and if they are not corrected, these negative traits could be your undoing. These negative habits or attitudes could gain control over you and hurt you before you realized that it was happening.

Let's create an example. Let's say you do not tidy up after yourself. Let's picture a terribly messy room and a terribly messy desk. Picture your clothes lying everywhere—on the bed, on the floor. Let's say wherever you go, you leave a mess. Now you may not realize it, but a lack of organization can cost you daily. The more disorganized you are, the longer it takes you to do anything. If you have to hunt for something you need, it takes time.

As a young student, a lack of organization can cost you time. You might be late for class or you might lose your homework in that messy environment. If you, looking wrinkled and disheveled, show up for class late without your homework, what impression are you giving others? Now, project yourself into the future 15 or 20 years. Do you think an employer is going to want to hire someone who cannot take care of himself? Do you think an employer is going to want to hire someone who looks unkempt, who would not be a good representative of a company? Probably not.

This is just an example of how one bad habit could possibly hurt you without your knowing it. If you know the negative parts of your life, you can do something to turn them into positive things, so your chances of success are greater.

To know your weaknesses is to know yourself well. As an adult, you will find that those who do the interviewing for jobs like candidates who know themselves so well that they can identify their own weaknesses. Does an interviewer want to know your weaknesses so you can be eliminated from competition? No, an interviewer wants to know if you know your own weaknesses and if you have a solution to resolve them so that you will be a better person.

Weaknesses or undesirable traits within oneself are to be accepted. However, negative traits or weaknesses are not to be permitted or encouraged to stay a part of one's life. Do something about bad habits or weaknesses or they will do something to you. Even the nasty habit of biting one's fingernails could keep one from getting a job if the interviewer does not like nail chewing.

It is a good thing to know the negative things about yourself. Knowing your bad habits means knowing what to do about them before your bad habits interfere with your success. Once you have taken an initial look at your positive and negative traits, you need to remind yourself that both the positive and negative traits make up who you are and you are important. You have come a long way in your accomplishments, achievements, and development even from just one year ago.

Career Search — CHAPTER 6: You are Unique, and That is Good

Name _____ Date _____

WHAT DO YOU THINK?

1. Name at least three things in your environment that you think make you the person you are today.
   _____
   _____

2. Name three of your interests and explain why you think you have these particular interests.
   _____
   _____
   _____
   _____

3. Describe your view of the world if everyone had the same talent.
   _____
   _____

4. Name three positive things about you that make you unique or different.
   _____
   _____

5. How do you feel about being unique or different from everyone else?
   _____
   _____

6. Name two friends and tell something about each that you think make them unique.
   _____
   _____
   _____

7. How would you feel if you were instructed to stop being unique and to start thinking and acting like your two friends?
   _____
   _____

8. List three things that you can do well, whether it is a sport, a hobby, or a school subject.
   _____
   _____

Career Search — CHAPTER 6: You are Unique, and That is Good

Name _____ Date _____

9. List three things you have heard other people say you do well.

_____
_____

10. Name three things that you see your friends doing but that you do not enjoy doing.

_____
_____

11. Name something about yourself that you would consider to be negative or a weakness and tell why it is negative.

_____
_____
_____

12. How could you change this negative into a positive or this weakness into a strength?

_____
_____
_____

13. If you could choose a unique talent or aptitude to be your own, what would it be? Explain your choice.

_____
_____
_____

14. List the talents of those in your family or with whom you are living.

_____
_____
_____
_____

15. Do you share a common talent or ability with any member of your family? If so, what is it?

_____
_____
_____

© Mark Twain Media, Inc., Publishers

CHAPTER 7
WHAT DO YOU THINK ABOUT YOU?

At this point in your physical and mental development, you may be involved in sports such as basketball, soccer, softball, volleyball, gymnastics, or swimming. You may be in the choir, band, or orchestra. By middle school you have learned to read and write, and you may have learned to write creatively and well. You understand math and science, and you have many interests and skills. It is all a part of your development.

By middle school you have experienced the early stages of career development. You have put aside your "dragon slayer" mode of thinking—or pretending. You have entered a realistic stage of career exploration. You are gathering information and are expressing preferences and values. You are moving in a progressive direction of career choice.

Mastering development tasks is very important because it allows you to move along to the next stage in your development. But mastering tasks in your development is important for another reason and that is your "self-concept."

When you accomplish tasks such as learning to ride a skateboard, learning to swim, or learning to do your math homework, you experience and observe something about yourself. You discover that you are capable, that you are able, that the brain in your head is working just as it should. The confidence you have gained through mastering the various tasks in your development enables you to go on to more difficult tasks. Simply put, the more you do, the more you realize you can do.

Think of this as a "three-do" cycle—the more you do, the more you realize you can do, so the more you do. This "three-do" cycle not only builds your self-confidence, it helps build your self-concept.

Your **self-concept** is your perception or your beliefs and ideas about yourself. Self-concept is how you see or consider yourself. Do you see yourself as capable, able, smart, intelligent, talented? Do you see yourself as someone who can learn, who can make friends easily, and who can achieve? Do you value yourself? These questions are posed for you so you can get an idea of your self-concept.

If your answers to the above questions about yourself were positive, undoubtedly you will move along in your development at a healthy pace. You also have a very good chance of success and a very good chance to achieve your dreams. Why? Because a self-concept is like your computer; it gives back to you the information you put into it. Your computer can only provide the information that was programmed into it. It is the same with your self-concept. If you believe you are capable, talented, and valuable, then those beliefs have gone into your self-concept and you will project to the world a positive self. On the other hand, negative input into your self-concept will result in your projecting to the world a negative self.

Think about it a moment. Who would make more friends, do the best in school, accomplish more tasks, be happier, and get the best jobs? Someone who projects a negative self or a positive self?

Everyone who is in school is capable, talented, and smart. Think for a moment about all the developmental tasks you have mastered since you were just a young child. Obviously, you are capable and able or you would not have mastered so many tasks by now. You must know how to read or you would not be reading this book. You must know how to listen or you would not be following your teacher's instructions.

Have you ever thought about what makes you smart and capable in the first place? It is a fact that you have this very complicated marvel, called a brain, in your head. Your brain is what allows you to do everything from control your own breathing, body temperature, and appetite to your physical movements and thoughts.

Billions of neurons constantly transmit information within and between the two hemispheres of your brain, which is designed so that parts of the brain cooperate with other parts, allowing you to walk, talk, think, feel, smell, see, remember, and recall information.

The left hemisphere of your brain participates in language functions—speaking, reading, and writing. The right hemisphere of your brain is associated with activity such as spatial analysis, face recognition, music appreciation, and sense of direction. And, interestingly enough, your hand movements are controlled by the opposite brain hemisphere. In other words, your left hand is controlled by your brain's right hemisphere and your right hand is controlled by your brain's left hemisphere.

The ability and complexity of the human brain is so very great that not even the most brilliant scientists have yet fully measured its capacity or function. With your brain and its infinite learning capacity, if you work at it, you can do just about anything that you choose to do because your brain is at your command. It will learn what you take the time to teach it.

Do you understand what a wonder you are? You have a brain at your command! You have a school curriculum that is designed and arranged to prepare you for your future and for the career of your dreams! You have the opportunity to explore and to find your unique career path! You are so important and valuable that your teachers want you to learn and to study, not so much so you will get an "A," but because your teachers want you to be the success that they know you can be.

You are a valuable person and your self-concept is your own, personal foundation that will keep you going as you maneuver through middle school, high school, and beyond. If you think and truly believe that you can do something, then you can. When you have a strong self-concept and you consider yourself to be worthy and deserving, you will have the self-esteem or the self-value that is needed to meet daily challenges. Then you will prepare yourself for opportunities that will come your way.

Take some time now and then to measure your self-concept. Oh, there will be days when you will not feel that you are the wonderful person who you are. That will pass. But, if you do not feel valuable, worthy, smart, capable, able, and likable most of the time, do something about it by talking with an adult. You do not want to risk passing up those exciting career opportunities that are going to come your way. If you are not watching for them, they could pass you by without your knowing it. An unhealthy self-concept could rob you of that fabulous future.

Your self-concept will develop as your skills, abilities, and achievements are acquired. The more you learn to do, the more self-confidence you will have. Remember the "three-do" cycle. It will help your self-concept.

One ability that you have acquired, which you may not have added to your list of developmental achievements, is the ability to **reason**. What is your reasoning ability? It is the process of thinking things through and beyond the obvious. Reasoning helps you to understand that there is more to learn than what is seen by the eye. It helps you to know more about yourself, about careers, about the world—about everything. Reasoning helps you to see and understand the depth and breadth of life.

As you begin your journey into the world of work and careers, the amount of information to which you are exposed is increasing, and the number of career choices that you are hearing and learning about is increasing, too. As a middle school student, you have made the transition from thinking about a few careers that have become familiar to you—doctor, lawyer, firefighter, police officer, teacher, and clergy. You are now beginning to hear and learn about the physical therapist, the botanist, chemical engineer, broker, psychologist, actuary, human resource manager, and more. This is when you use your reasoning ability.

As a young child, you learned through experiences and observation. For example, when you were just an infant, if your caregiver walked out of the room, you probably thought she or he was gone forever or that she or he had disappeared. Today, if your teacher walks out of the classroom, your reasoning ability tells you that your teacher will return. Your reasoning also tells you that your teacher is not a school building fixture, but that your teacher lives somewhere other than at the school.

Reasoning ability is important in career development and planning. If you did not have the ability to reason, you would not understand that there are careers within the cluster or field of a career. Remember the career "umbrella"? Without reasoning you would not understand that under the "umbrella" of nursing, there are many types of nursing and that a nurse is more than just the nurse one sees on television who wears a white dress and white cap and sometimes administers injections. In fact, a nurse very well could be a man, since a number of men, today, choose nursing as their career.

Today, under the profession or umbrella of nursing, there is pediatric nursing, psychiatric nursing, geriatric nursing, home health care nursing, cardiac care nursing, intensive care nursing, and more.

Reasoning helps you when you begin your career path. In high school, you will be able to choose your classes. If you are planning to attend college, you will need to select challenging courses. In college, as you select courses and a major (those classes which are focused upon a specific field of study), you will need to reason or understand which courses would be applicable to various careers.

For example, suppose a college student had a talent for math and wanted to major in math. Reason would help the student understand that majoring in math would enable the student to obtain a career that required math skills. The student would, after learning in middle school about careers, know that math skills could be applied to a career as a teacher or a scientist, a pilot, a statistician, an underwriter, an actuary, an accountant, a business manager, a broker, and many other careers.

Reasoning applies to understanding yourself, too. You are not just a middle school student. There are many facets or sides to you. In addition to being a student, you may be a musician, scout, collector, gardener, cheerleader, neighbor, pet owner, cousin, athlete, artist, church or synagogue member, and so on.

Your reasoning skills will aid you in your career development as well as your personal development. You will need to go beyond just hearing the titles or names of careers. You will need to do your own searching to find out the aptitudes, abilities, and education required for careers in which you are interested.

Your reasoning ability will allow you to see yourself as more than one-dimensional. With reasoning, you can understand that you are a multifaceted (many-sided) person with talents, preferences, contributions, and ideas. With reason, eventually you will see how all these sides of you can match up with all facets or sides of a specific career that requires the talents, abilities, and personal strengths of someone like you.

Name _____ Date _____

WHAT DO YOU THINK?

1. Have you recently learned a new skill, a game, an instrument, or a new subject in school? If yes, what did you learn?
   _____
   _____

2. Did you teach yourself this new skill or did someone teach you, or both?
   _____
   _____

3. How long did it take you to learn or master this new skill?
   _____
   _____

4. How do you feel about yourself after you learn a new skill or subject?
   _____
   _____

5. If your self-concept is your belief about yourself, explain how you feel about yourself. What do you think about yourself?
   _____
   _____
   _____

6. Name three things that have a strong effect on your belief about yourself.
   _____
   _____

7. Name three things that you can do to maintain a strong self-concept.
   _____
   _____

8. Name three things that could weaken your self-concept.
   _____
   _____
   _____

Career Search CHAPTER 7: What Do You Think About You?

Name _____ Date _____

9. How would you describe someone who had a weak, poor self-concept?

_____

_____

_____

10. How would you describe someone who had a strong, healthy self-concept?

_____

_____

_____

11. Explain how your self-concept affects your school performance.

_____

_____

_____

12. Explain the effect of self-concept upon a career.

_____

_____

_____

13. Describe the many facets or sides of you.

_____

_____

_____

14. Explain the many facets or sides of one of your parents or your caregiver.

_____

_____

_____

15. List the career opportunities under the umbrella or within the cluster of "art."

_____

_____

_____

CHAPTER 8
WHAT MAKES YOU TICK?

You are now aware of your self-concept, or your set of beliefs about yourself. While we are on the subject, let us spend a little more time talking about you. It is important for you to know what makes you "tick"—to know your own beliefs, values, preferences, likes, dislikes, and so on.

Why is this information important? It is important to not only know yourself so you can understand and accept who you are, but self-knowledge also is important in your career decision.

Some experts believe that if you can find out enough about yourself and then find out enough about careers, you could make a perfect match.

You make a match by knowing your characteristics, your values, likes, wants, needs, and things you do not want or like. For example, if you are prone to sea sickness, you obviously would not want to become a sailor. If you have allergies to plants, horticulture would probably not be the career for you. If you do not like math, accounting should be left to those who do. If you are painfully shy, perhaps you would not wish to consider a career as a hotel concierge. But, there is even more to making a career match than knowing about one's allergies and a tendency to be shy.

Describe and understand the environment in which you want to work and then learn as much as you can about the careers that provide the kind of working environment you desire. Do you want to work independently or as a team member? Do you want to work outdoors or indoors, at a desk or in a laboratory? Do you want to teach students or do you want to train animals? Do you want to work in complete silence or do you want to be around people? You decide what appeals to you and then find out what careers would provide the environment in which you are interested.

While all this sounds relatively simple, like a small effort that could be completed in minutes, gaining knowledge about yourself and about the infinite number of careers is a task that requires a lot of work completed over a lengthy period of time, which is why you should begin today.

Learning about yourself is fun because you are a very interesting, unique, special, valuable person. No kidding! When was the last time you had a really good thought about yourself? When was the last time you thought, "Hey! I really am a unique person. I am capable of many things. I can do a lot of things very well."? Has it been some time since you had a positive thought about yourself? Well, why not take a few seconds and give yourself a "pat on the back." Stop what you are doing this very minute. Yes, stop and put the pen or pencil down. Now, pat yourself on the back and say aloud, yes aloud, "**I AM A GREAT PERSON AND I CAN DO GREAT THINGS!**"

Excellent! Now, moving right along. . . .

Part of knowing who you are is knowing your personal values. **Personal values** are those ideals and beliefs that a person strives for or works to uphold and demonstrate in daily life. Personal values serve as a foundation for one's direction in life.

Careers are selected, in part, by your personal values. This is why it is essential to understand what values are important to you. Values can and should be incorporated into your career planning. The values that guide your life are manifested or made evident through your career choices.

For example, if your values include helpfulness, hard work, and responsibility, you might consider careers in medicine, law, law enforcement, criminal justice, health care, education, or government. If compassion, helpfulness, and good health are your values, you might consider a career as a personal trainer, aerobics instructor, health club manager, nurse, therapist, minister, social worker, counselor, or dietitian.

Since careers in general are designed to help society, or to make the world go 'round, most positive values would apply to most careers. However, it is important to your career happiness to know what institutions, ideals, and customs you esteem or value. Matching your values to careers that best represent your values will help create the right working environment for you.

If you consider the many careers and professions in existence, you would see that careers are a way of allowing an individual to express his or her values. Going back to some of the famous people listed in a previous chapter, their careers and career choices seem appropriate, given each of their reported values.

Sojourner Truth, the famous abolitionist (one who works to exterminate or stamp out something), valued compassion, freedom, and the institution of religion, as well as the institution of family. She was a mother of five children, and she was an evangelist. Her purpose and her values were manifested, or made known, through her work.

Albert Einstein, a physicist, valued teaching and learning. It has been written that Dr. Einstein had difficulty adapting to formal schooling as a child. It was on his own that he developed his deep curiosity for math. His passion for math led to his continued interest in his work, resulting in his major achievement, the theory of relativity. Dr. Einstein's value of learning was manifested in his long career as a teacher of physics and mathematics. His value of human life was manifested in his efforts toward world peace during the time of World War II.

What are your values? Are your values being manifested through your work today? You can get a good idea of your personal values by paying attention to how you spend your time, how you live, and how you spend your money. If you work to improve your school, responsibility and respect would be some of your values. If you help others, respect, kindness, and helpfulness would be some of your values.

If you spend most of your time in school and studying, then you value education and learning. If, on the other hand, you spend most of your time sleeping, watching television, or "goofing around," you are demonstrating that you do not place too much value on education. The same principle can be applied to your money. Pay attention to how you consistently use and spend your money and you will see what it is that you value. Where you put your time and money are generally where your personal values lie.

Where do we get our original values? Usually our values come from those with whom we live on a day-to-day basis. When you were younger, did you ever hear your parents or caregiver remind you to "say thank you," or to "be polite"? If so, then you were exposed to a sign of respect, and respect is a value. Have you ever been reminded to clean your room or to write neatly? Neatness is a value.

As a young child, one does not have the ability to recognize or study the importance or effect of a value upon one's life. When you were instructed to clean your room, did you stop and think that learning neatness would help you become a more organized, efficient, and effective individual as an adult? Probably not.

Usually without question, a young child will incorporate or adopt a parent's or caregiver's values. But as a child grows older and matures, he or she may begin to question those values that were taught to him or her long ago. As a young child, Susie was taught to save part of her money and to put it in the bank. Now, as a middle school-aged girl, Susie does not like the idea of putting her money in the bank. She wants to spend it and spend it all. She questions her parents as to why she must save her money.

When a child begins to question the values taught to him or her in earlier years, this is the child's way of "individuating" or transferring those values taught by parents and many times making those values his or her own. Once Susie talks with her parents about her money, she may fully understand why it makes good sense to save her money. Then Susie can eventually decide for herself where her money goes, making that value of "financial health" a value of her own.

To know your personal values is to know who you are and why you do what you do, or . . . what makes you tick. If you take violin or piano lessons or if you are in the school band, you know that you value music. If you are a member of a church or synagogue, you know that you value the institution of religion. If you are a member of a sports team, you know that you value team participation and perhaps physical health, sportsmanship, and fellowship.

If you are spending your time doing something that you do not like to do, or if you are spending your time doing things that do not represent your values, perhaps you should rethink your time and activities. To have values that are important to you and to be involved in those activities that represent your values will add harmony and balance to your life and allow you to build upon your foundation of personal integrity and purpose.

Check your values. You may be more purposeful, conscientious, helpful, caring, and concerned than you ever realized.

There are other values besides just personal values. There are **universal values**, or those ideas, beliefs, or concepts about the world that are not only important to you, but are shared by other people around the globe. While personal values are values you feel are unique to you, universal values are common to societies in addition to our own.

The sanctity of life is a universal value. It is a value upheld by those of us who live in the United States as well as by societies in Europe, Africa, Asia, and elsewhere. The sanctity of life is so very dear to us and people around the world that many people dedicate their lives to saving the lives of other people.

Mother Teresa, who lived and died in India, gave her life to loving and helping the very poor. Princess Diana of England worked for numerous charities and causes that benefitted society. Before her death in 1997, Princess Diana was working to eliminate land mines that were killing residents in post-war zones. Martin Luther King worked for equal rights in behalf of African Americans and peace for everyone.

Do you know your universal values? You may have worked for a worthy cause and not realized that your work was due to your personal and universal values. Have you picked up litter around your neighborhood or school? Have you collected cans for a food drive? Have you gathered soda cans for recycling? Have you written a poem or essay about a universal value such as freedom or peace? All those efforts are related to universal values.

There are many universal values that motivate us to help make the world go 'round, or to make the world a better place to live. If you consider your universal values, you can find many related concerns and causes in which you can get involved. You can eventually focus a career upon a need related to universal values.

If quality of life for mankind is one of your universal values, many careers exist in which you can incorporate your values. Careers in religion, science, medicine, agriculture, space exploration, space technology, oceanography, and education are just a few in which you can work to make the world a better place in which to live. If the environment is one of your universal values, you could consider a career in agriculture, forestry, physical science, chemistry, geology, geography, architecture, archeology, astronomy, conservation, environmental law, or engineering.

When you define or articulate your values, you can match them with a career in which your values can be utilized. If your universal values are made manifest, like those of Dr. King, Princess Diana, and Mother Teresa, if your universal values are utilized and demonstrated through your career choice, your chances of personal and career satisfaction are much greater. You can help yourself and the world at the same time by putting your values to work.

A third group of important values are **career values**. These are ideas, beliefs, and priorities that are important to career satisfaction. People choose careers for a number of reasons and many of them are based upon what are referred to as career values.

Many people consider salary or earning power a career value. Generally, though, most people do not consider the amount of money earned as their number one career value. Career values most people consider are: job security or the assurance of continued employment within a career, being part of a team or working with others, the opportunity for expressing one's creativity, the opportunity for status, the opportunity for personal growth and development, independence or the opportunity to work without extended supervision, company benefits, technical support, a variety of work, child care, hours required to do the work, life balance, continued educational opportunities, job location, recognition and promotion, work environment, travel opportunities, company integrity (or the company's reputation for fairness, honesty, and product or service quality) and, last but not least, the opportunity to express one's values.

Mr. Jones was ready to apply for a job as an editor for a publishing company. He had to consider the work environment at the publishing company since Mr. Jones knew that he worked best and concentrated better when he could have absolute silence. Mr. Jones also knew that he would not work for any publishing company that published books that were in conflict with his personal values of the institution of family.

Because Mr. Jones was, basically, a writer, he knew that he would have to have the room or the freedom to express his creativity. For personal information, Mr. Jones researched the company with which he was going to interview, since company integrity was high on his list.

Salary was definitely a career value to Mr. Jones, but it was not the number one career value. Frankly, the character and attitude of his boss was a major career value to Mr. Jones. He wanted to work for someone who had values similar to his own. Mr. Jones was pleased to discover the company for which he was going to interview contributed a good deal of money to various charities. To Mr. Jones, this company sounded like a winner. He approached his interview with greater enthusiasm than he would otherwise have.

Remember to consider your career values when you research careers. And, when pondering or thinking about career choice, the more your values—personal, universal, and career—match those of the career, the better chance for career satisfaction. To make a career decision without considering your values could lead to discontent, unhappiness, and frustration.

Name _____ Date _____

WHAT DO YOU THINK?

1. Name at least three of your personal values.
_____
_____

2. Where or how do you think you acquired these values?
_____
_____
_____

3. How do these values guide your life?
_____
_____
_____

4. What famous person, in the past or present, represents values that you think are similar to yours? Name the person and the values that you have in common.
_____
_____

5. Name a friend who has values similar to your own.
_____

6. How do you spend your after-school time? What value or values do you think you are representing by the way you spend your time?
_____
_____
_____

7. Do you belong to any organizations, clubs, or teams? If so, what values does your team or club represent?
_____
_____
_____

Name _____ Date _____

8. List some of your parents' or family's values that you have incorporated as your own. Explain why you now view these values as your own.

_____

_____

_____

9. List three of your universal values.

_____

_____

10. Explain why these three values you listed are important to the world and also why they are important to you.

_____

_____

_____

_____

11. Name a good career choice for each value you listed in exercise number 9 and explain your career choices.

_____

_____

_____

_____

12. Would any of the careers you selected in exercise number 11 require a college degree? If so, which career(s)?

_____

_____

13. Do you know someone whose work represents universal values? If yes, name the person, his or her work, and the value that is represented by this work.

_____

_____

_____

_____

Career Search CHAPTER 8: What Makes You Tick?

Name _____ Date _____

14. Former President Jimmy Carter and the former First Lady, Mrs. Carter, have volunteered much of their time to Habitat for Humanity, an organization that provides housing to people in need. What organization or cause would interest you and allow you to express your universal values?

_____

_____

_____

15. If housing for the needy were one's universal value, what career would be a good choice for someone who possessed this value? Explain your choice.

_____

_____

_____

16. Get a newspaper and note the ads of job opportunities that describe your career values. Either clip the ad and attach to this worksheet or simply write out the ad.

_____

_____

_____

17. What career values are implied or stated in the ad that you selected?

_____

_____

18. List three careers that have your career values. Write one career value next to the career listed.

_____

_____

_____

19. Name one person you know who is employed in one of the three careers you listed in exercise number 18.

_____

20. Name three career values that you think a career in teaching represents.

_____

_____

© Mark Twain Media, Inc., Publishers

CHAPTER 9
TESTING. TESTING. 1 . . . 2 . . . 3 . . .

By the time you reach middle school, you may have considered joining some activities or organizations such as choir, a theater group, a babysitters' club, or a school-sponsored activity such as band or sports. In fact, there may be many groups and teams that you would like to join, but you know that you do not have enough time to participate in all of them.

Career choice is a similar dilemma. Given the thousands of careers from which to choose and all the interests you have, you know that even an entire lifetime would not give you enough time to pursue each and every career. Choosing a career out of the thousands in existence is a difficult process for some young adults, but not unlike the process you would use in choosing after-school activities as a middle school student.

When selecting school organizations and activities, you probably consider joining the ones with which you have something in common. If you play an instrument, you might join the band. If you like hiking, field trips, and learning different skills, you might join scouting. You choose your groups because you have something in common with the group. You eliminate the groups or activities with which you have very little or nothing in common. You would not join a sports team if you did not play sports and had no intention of ever playing sports. You would not join the marching band if all you ever wanted to play was the violin.

Because you do not have enough spare time to join everything, you use a simple process of elimination. Why is it simple? Choosing groups, organizations, and clubs at school is rather easy because you usually know what clubs, groups, organizations, or activities are available to you and what they are all about. And, most times, you know some of the members.

Why could you not use the simple process of elimination when selecting a career path? Frankly, you could if you knew enough information about every single career in existence. But really knowing about a career means knowing what education and training are required, knowing what skills and personality would fit, knowing the experience and qualifications required, knowing what work is performed and what responsibilities are held by the person who enters the career, and knowing what advancement opportunities would be available to the person going into the career.

Not knowing about a career is the same as eliminating one of your career choices. Not knowing yourself well enough to match yourself with a career is the same as eliminating some, if not many, career choices.

So, what can you do? Can you rush to study about every career? Can you begin an in-depth analysis of yourself? How would you go about doing either one? How long would it take for you to learn all you would need to know about every career in the world and to learn, in depth, about yourself in order to make a qualified, sound, accurate career choice?

A long time, maybe? Yes, a very, VERY, long time. That is, unless you turned to career testing.

Career testing is used by career counselors to measure or assess various parts of career choice. These tests, depending on what the counselor is measuring or assessing, are called by many different names. Some are called inventories, some are called assessments, some are called searches, evaluations, vocational guidance instruments, and, of course, career tests. But you need not worry; you do not receive a grade for these kinds of tests, and you cannot fail them when you take them.

Today there are numerous tests or inventories available that can help you discover more about yourself and more about the kinds of careers that appeal to you. These instruments or tests are used for determining factors such as whether or not you would be successful in a certain profession or career, to what extent your character matches or is similar to the character of those people already working in a certain profession or career, how knowledgeable you are about careers and the world of careers in general, and what you have learned about careers and how you have used that career information.

Career tests are not created to give you magic formulas or instant answers. Sometimes students get the idea that career tests are the "genie in the bottle," or shortcuts to career development. The fact is, there is no substitute for career development. Often to the disappointment of many, career tests do not and should not select a career for anyone. One reason tests are not designed to select the career for an individual is because many people are suited for more than just one career, and the choice of career should be left up to the individual.

The overall objective of career tests is to help one find and select a career cluster or career field that would allow an individual the expression of their talents, abilities, and interests. The purpose of career tests is to help one acquire self-knowledge so that intelligent career choices can be identified. With the results of career testing, a trained career counselor can help guide one along his or her career development journey.

Career tests can provide information such as an individual's personality profile, how similar an individuals' interests are with those who are performing within a certain career environment, a measurement of one's aptitudes or natural talents, a measurement of one's abilities such as math, language, reasoning, and spelling skills, and one's occupational interests.

While the thought of actually taking a career test may sound intimidating, keep in mind that there is no grade and that the results are tools to use for your benefit. Some career tests are available as early as elementary school, but most are available to those in the eighth grade and beyond. More and more, schools are creating career programs that provide access to career testing, giving students the opportunity to plan their career future.

With hundreds, perhaps thousands, of testing instruments available today, it is not possible in this publication to list and discuss them all. However, a brief description of a few vocational guidance instruments will help you become familiar with those that are more widely used.

The Myer-Briggs Type Indicator is, basically, an assessment of personality types. Often referred to as the MBTI, this test is used to determine your personal style. Are you more introverted or extroverted? Are you more intuitive or logical? Can you "fail" an MBTI test? No. The results of an MBTI are helpful to you in that you can compare your personality style to the personality style most often found within a particular career or profession.

Your occupational or career interests can be measured by a test called the Strong Interest Inventory, which was, in the past, called the Strong-Campbell Interest Inventory or the Strong Vocational Interest Blank. Sometimes referred to as the SII, this instrument measures interests and how similar your interests are with those people who find satisfaction within various careers.

A series of aptitude tests conducted by the Johnson O'Connor Research Foundation are designed to test or measure your natural abilities or aptitudes. These tests do not consist of questions, and they do not indicate your interests. Aptitude testing at Johnson O'Connor Research Foundation measures things about a person with which you may not be familiar, things like the client's visual perception, divergent thinking, convergent thinking, number facilitation, structural visualization, tonal memory, pitch discrimination, rhythm memory, finger dexterity, subjective or objective personality, and more. This information can then help the client identify the careers that use his or her aptitudes.

Knowing your aptitudes can provide a logical and practical answer as to why certain careers are more appealing and rewarding to you. Those at the Johnson O'Connor Research Foundation believe that unused aptitudes can cause frustration. Therefore, the key is to learn your aptitudes and select the career in which you can use them.

The Johnson O'Connor Research Foundation emphasizes that knowing your aptitudes is of utmost importance when it comes to your happiness. However, the Foundation and its representatives have stressed that one must acquire knowledge in order to achieve success. This means that even if you have the natural aptitudes of a scientist, a doctor, a teacher, or a metallurgical analyst, you must acquire the appropriate knowledge, education, and training to be a success.

There is enough evidence to question students' tendencies to neglect planning their future careers. Career testing is helpful in improving one's career future by allowing a student to consider what they want out of life and to clarify steps needed to take in order to discover how they can get from "here" to "there." Testing allows investigation, identification, and recognition of one's own personality traits, interests, aptitudes, attitudes, values, and special needs, if any, that will help one succeed.

It is no secret that choosing an educational and career path without knowing the reason why can cost a student money, time, grief, and a great deal of unhappiness. Career testing allows the student to know one's self and to know why a particular career and educational path is logical, practical, or makes sense. This prevents future regrets over career choices.

It was Ralph Waldo Emerson, a poet, who once stated, "The crowning fortune of a man is to be born to some pursuit which finds him employment and happiness, whether it be to make baskets, or broadswords, or canals, or statues, or songs." To find your "crowning fortune," add career testing to your career development just for the sake of your own happiness.

The author of Ecclesiastes, after decades of searching for the meaning of life, wrote, "That everyone may . . . find satisfaction in all his toil—this is the gift of God." Your gift of satisfaction in your work awaits you. Consider career testing to help you find it.

In addition to taking various tests, begin studying about various careers and the requirements of each. Given the number of careers in existence, this activity can, of course, be done over time. But, a good time to start is today. Reading in detail about a variety of careers allows you the opportunity to daydream, to imagine yourself in any particular career role.

After you have been assessed or tested through a career test, you will, most often, be given the results on paper after a guidance counselor or the person who tested you explains your test results. In addition to various career tests or assessments, it is also important for you to spend time assessing yourself. While you know yourself better than anyone, actually writing down self-information allows you to recognize your own personal traits, values, skills, and more. By supplementing career tests with your own personal assessment, you are helping yourself move along the career development path at a good pace. Once you know your own traits, you can play a matching game, if you will, with the careers about which you have read and studied. Try it and see how many "matches" you make. You may be surprised!

Career Search   CHAPTER 9: Testing. Testing. 1 . . . 2 . . . 3 . . .

Name _____ Date _____

WHAT DO YOU THINK?

1. Name the clubs, teams, organizations, or youth groups to which you belong.
_____
_____
_____

2. Tell how you decided to join these particular groups.
_____
_____
_____
_____

3. If you had to choose a career today, how would you do it?
_____
_____
_____
_____

4. What kind of information do you think you could learn from a career test?
_____
_____
_____
_____

5. Would you consider taking a career test? Why or why not?
_____
_____
_____

6. Name two advantages of taking a career test.
_____
_____
_____

Name _____ Date _____

7. Can you think of any disadvantages of taking a career test?

_____
_____
_____

8. Do you think students should spend more or less time studying careers? Explain your answer.

_____
_____
_____

9. How could career testing help a student who is graduating from high school and is planning to enter college?

_____
_____
_____

10. Why would it be unwise to assume that a career test will identify the one career for you?

_____
_____
_____

11. If a career test indicated your values, interests, and aptitudes were compatible with the legal profession, what would be the next step in your career development process?

_____
_____
_____
_____

CHAPTER 10
POLLY WANTS A CRACKER

When adults take road trips in their cars, they sometimes use road maps because they want to get to their destination. They want to get from where they are to where they are going. Getting "there" is their goal, so they plan their trip by using a map. They spend their time choosing the best route to travel in order to reach their goal, which is their destination.

A **goal** is that into which you put your effort and energy. On a road map, where you want to arrive is your goal. In career development, the career you desire is your goal. However, getting to any destination takes time. Some goals take longer to achieve than others.

Have you ever heard a parrot squawk, "Polly wants a cracker!"? The parrot's goal is a cracker. She wants that cracker, and she wants it now. Polly is a bird. She cannot make a plan or come up with a methodical way to achieve her goal, the cracker. Because she cannot plan, Polly is dependent upon someone to give her the cracker.

If you do not set goals and make plans to meet those goals, you will not be much different than a squawking parrot. You will be dependent upon others who will decide what is best for you. Like Polly who sometimes gets a cracker, you will have to take what you get if you fail to set and reach goals.

Toddlers or preschoolers have short-term or immediate goals. When toddlers want something, it is usually soon or now—not next week or next year. If a toddler is hungry, he or she will go about achieving the immediate goal of getting a slice of apple or a cookie. The toddler might tug on the caregiver's clothing or the toddler might even begin to cry. We cannot expect a toddler to wait for lunch time or dinner time because time has very little meaning to a two- or three-year-old child. Therefore, a long-term goal, to a very young child, is inconceivable or meaningless.

You, on the other hand, have developed reasoning ability. You know that time does have meaning. Therefore, you can make plans and you can list goals. You know that time will pass and tomorrow, next week, next month, and next year will surely come.

Most successful people make both short-term and long-term goals. Some people write their goals down so that they will be reminded of the things they must do in order to achieve their goals. Those things that must be done in order to achieve a goal are goals, too—short-term or intermediate goals.

A **short-term goal** is, of course, a goal that is to be achieved within a short period of time. A goal to be achieved this evening or even next week is a short-term goal. **Intermediate goals** are those goals, sometimes short-term, that are achieved before long-term goals are achieved. **Long-term goals** can take a month to a year, or one to 30 years, or even a lifetime to achieve. Short-term or intermediate goals are necessary to help you reach your long-term goals.

If you want to achieve the long-term goal of a college degree, you must at first plan an intermediate goal of a high school diploma. A short-term goal of studying and doing your homework each day would help you achieve your intermediate goal of a high school diploma. The high school diploma, or intermediate goal, will help you achieve your college degree.

Achieved goals are the result of careful planning. Many successful people plan their lives by goals. By listing your goals, you will learn more about yourself, your wants, and your desires. When thinking about short- and long-term goals, you are helping yourself create your own personal "road map." You are helping yourself learn the direction you want to go in your life. **Defined goals**, or those goals that are articulated, described, or written down, serve a purpose in that they remind you of where you want to go in your life—tomorrow, next week, next year, or in the next 10 years.

Have you ever wanted something so badly that you spent a lot of time thinking about how you were going to get it? Selecting a goal and planning a way to achieve it is an example of goal setting. Perhaps you are planning to have a party one week from today at your house, and you want your house to be tidy when your friends arrive. You set aside the approaching weekend for housecleaning. Your intermediate goal is a clean house, and your time frame is one week.

Maybe you want a new car by the time you graduate from high school. You decide that you can earn money by babysitting and mowing lawns during the summers. Your goal is a car and your time frame is several years from now. This is a long-term goal. Finding jobs during the summer could be short-term or long-term goals, but they are smaller, more immediate goals to achieve before you can achieve your big, long-term goal of buying a car.

Setting a goal and achieving it is similar to driving along a road, the road to your goal. The road will not always be smooth. There may be bumps, curves, potholes, and dips in the road. Some road maps will tell you where some of those little surprises—the curves and the hills—are located, but most do not have information about bumps and potholes.

If your goal is to have that new car by the time you leave high school, there are many things that could get in your way between now and then. You may earn some money and then lose it. You may earn lots of money for the car and then spend it on something else. Your parents may initially disapprove of your having a car when you graduate from high school. You won't know what is going to happen until it happens, so you must be prepared for problems to arise when you set goals. And, you must be prepared to keep working toward your goal, even if you experience problems.

To achieve a goal, you must keep going and not let the rough road become a deterrent or a "road block," even if it means taking another road, path, or avenue. To achieve a goal, you must keep your goal in mind and keep going until you get there, regardless of the obstacles. If your goal is worthwhile, if your goal is very important to you, and if you can stay focused on your goal and keep going, then you will achieve it.

Most successful people try this goal-setting method. They choose their goal. They write it down. Then they write down immediate goals or those goals that must be accomplished before they can reach their major or long-term goal. Sometimes they imagine how they would look when they achieve the goal. They see themselves achieving it, winning it, or making it.

Goal-oriented Olympic athletes talk about seeing themselves up on the winner's podium, accepting the gold medal as the national anthem is playing. They imagine themselves waving at the cheering crowd as the cameras flash, and the newspaper reporters line up for interviews. These Olympic athletes keep this image in their minds as they train day after day, month after month, and even year after year. They know their goal—a gold medal. They know what is expected of a gold-medal winner—months and years of training. So they work hard and train hard because that image of winning keeps them going. They can almost feel that gold medal hanging around their neck! They can almost hear their national anthem! They can almost see a crowd of cheering, smiling, excited people! So they keep working and working towards their goal until they succeed.

What happens if you do not plan or set career goals? First of all, you are taking a great risk. Failing to plan and make career goals is similar to naming a faraway city as your destination and then setting out on the trip with no road map or guide. With just the assumption that you will arrive at your destination, you fail to find out how much fuel, money, food, and time you will need. You fail to check the engine, oil, or tires. Your arrival is very important to your family; they are waiting for you at the other end. But without adequate resources or a road map, what do you think your chances of arriving are?

Dreaming about a career or a comfortable life in which you make the decisions for yourself is time foolishly spent if you do not plan and set goals. Why would you start off on an automobile trip to a place you have never been without a road map? Why would you, then, enroll in a college, a college which costs a lot of money, if you do not have the slightest idea if the course work is suited for you?

The biggest risk you take when failing to plan and set career goals is your happiness. Without setting goals and planning to achieve them, you are setting yourself up to be a squawking parrot who has to settle for whatever is handed to you.

Putting it simply, failing to plan is planning to fail. Know your goals and make plans. Set goals that will enable you to achieve that career of your dreams. Frankly, the world needs the benefit of your success.

Career Search · CHAPTER 10: Polly Wants a Cracker

Name _____ Date _____

WHAT DO YOU THINK?

1. List three long-term goals that you have set for yourself.

_____
_____
_____
_____

2. List three short-term or intermediate goals that will help you reach your long-term goals.

_____
_____
_____
_____

3. What is the purpose of goal-setting?

_____
_____
_____

4. If you had a long-term goal of traveling to another country someday, what short-term or intermediate goals would you set?

_____
_____
_____
_____

5. If you desire a comfortable, successful life as an adult, what should be some of your goals?

_____
_____
_____
_____
_____

Name _____ Date _____

6. If your goal is to find the right career for yourself, what would be your short-term or intermediate goals?

_____

_____

_____

_____

7. Would you need help in achieving this long-term goal?

_____

Who or what can help you achieve this long-term goal?

_____

_____

_____

8. To have your room cleaned by tomorrow or to finish a book by next week are short-term goals. List two short-term goals you would like to accomplish.

_____

_____

_____

_____

9. If you were an Olympic skier, how would you use visualization to achieve your goal of winning a gold medal?

_____

_____

_____

_____

10. Why is it a waste of time to dream about a career if you do not plan and set goals?

_____

_____

_____

_____

CHAPTER 11
HEALTHY OR TOXIC; POSITIVE OR NEGATIVE: THE CHOICE IS YOURS

As you progress through career development, decision-making becomes your privilege and your responsibility. Most middle school students think this is exhilarating; at long last you get to make some decisions on your own. Many of you will make healthy decisions regarding your present and your future. Some of you, if you are not aware, could make toxic decisions.

Since the decision-making process about your life will ultimately become your own, you need to understand two basic points: one, you can make positive choices that will help you; and two, you can make negative choices that will harm you.

Healthy choices in your life will lend strength to your success, while **toxic choices** in your life will have a negative, bad, or unhealthy effect on you.

In setting career goals, it seems reasonable that you would want to make healthy choices. Toxic choices can deter you or keep you from your goal. If your career goal is to become a teacher or a dancer or a coach, healthy choices made by you will get you closer to your objective.

The number of decisions set before middle school students can be overwhelming. Becoming aware of your healthy choices and your toxic choices is vital to your health, wellness, and overall success. All the career planning in the world will not matter if you are unaware of the kinds of choices you are making.

If your goal is to make a good grade on the next test, skipping class on a test day is a toxic or an unhealthy choice. If your goal is to make the basketball or volleyball team, being a bully on the court or playing unfairly is a toxic choice. Awareness of the choices you are making will increase the number of healthy choices you make and reduce the number of toxic choices you make. Healthy choices mean greater chances for success and fewer chances for failure.

Healthy choices mean rejecting or not choosing toxic choices such as drugs, tobacco, alcohol, and premarital sex. These substances and behaviors can not only cost you your health and career success, but they also have the potential to cost you your life.

If you are unaware of how the chemicals in drugs, alcohol, and tobacco negatively affect your brain and your body, talk with a trusted adult. If you are not convinced that sex and the potential for pregnancy and sexually transmitted diseases exist, talk with a trusted adult.

Middle school students should know the facts about drugs, alcohol, tobacco, and sex. If you want to make the decisions regarding your life, you must accept the responsibility for your decisions. You make the decisions in your life. You are responsible for your behavior. You are responsible for your body. The results of your decisions will be yours to live with for the rest of your life.

If you are participating in drugs, alcohol, tobacco, or premarital sex, **STOP**. Any or all of these substances or behaviors can present problems for you beyond your ability to solve, even with help from an adult.

Healthy and toxic choices can apply to the company you keep—your friends. A healthy choice in friends is choosing friends who make healthy choices in their lives. A toxic choice is choosing friends who make toxic choices in their lives. If your friend is one who cheats on exams, drinks alcohol, or steals, you have made a toxic choice in a friend. If your friend is one who generally makes healthy lifestyle choices, then you have made a healthy choice in a friend.

Experts called "behaviorists" have theorized that young people tend to do the same thing that they observe in others. Big businesses create products based on this theory. Toy manufacturers have successfully built businesses making toy lawn mowers, chemistry sets, tables and chairs, toy washers and dryers, powered mini-cars, and even toy people, or dolls. Children like to imitate others' behavior. Toy manufacturers bank their money on it.

Consider your choices in friends. Are you doing what someone else is doing without thinking it through or without considering the consequences? Are your friends healthy or toxic, a positive or a negative influence on you? It seems reasonable that you would want to choose wisely those friends whose behavior models healthy, sound behavior since their influence could easily affect your life and your future.

Gangs would not exist today if people did not imitate behavior. Gang members do not think for themselves; they only do what someone else tells them to do or what they see someone else doing. Unfortunately, gang members are turning their decision-making over to someone else. If you turn your decision-making over to someone else, you might as well go ahead and turn your future over to them, too, because if someone makes a toxic choice for you, you are at risk and are responsible.

There is a simple truth in the saying, "If you play, you pay." Far too many young people have experienced this lesson the hard way. There are enough documented cases of young, drunk drivers losing control and killing every passenger in their car and sometimes in another car, too. Choosing to ride with someone who is drinking is not only a toxic choice, but it could turn out to be a fatal choice for you, too. If you have a friend who has been drinking and gets behind the wheel of a car, make a healthy choice for you and for your friend. Take the keys.

Make healthy, positive choices regarding friends. Choose positive friends who make healthy choices for themselves. Do not put your future at risk by associating with friends who make toxic choices. Your future, even your life, could depend upon the company you keep. Your life depends upon the choices you make.

Make healthy choices in your everyday life—food, work, play, and behavior. Far too many students cut their futures short by making quick, hasty, thoughtless, toxic choices. Today there are young people who speak on high school and college campuses about sex, drugs, and drinking. Some of these speakers have AIDS as a result of unprotected sex, and they now spend time trying to warn other students what can happen as a result of a foolish choice. Some speakers have survived horrible car accidents in which people were killed because the speaker was, at the time of the accident, driving while drunk.

Be informed or be at risk. The choice is yours. Remember this: it is easier to stay out of toxic situations and away from toxic behaviors in the first place than it is to get out of it later. Make healthy choices and make plans for a beautiful future.

Name _____ Date _____

WHAT DO YOU THINK?

1. Name three healthy foods that you like to eat.
_____
_____

2. Are there any healthy foods that you do not like, but you eat them because they are good for you?
_____
_____

3. Name three healthy things that you do to stay strong and energetic.
_____
_____

4. Name three toxic things that, if you were to indulge in them, would be toxic to you and your future.
_____
_____

5. Is driving a car beyond the speed limit a healthy or a toxic choice? Explain.
_____
_____

6. What are the advantages of being with friends who make healthy choices in their lives?
_____
_____

7. What would be the risks of being with a friend who engages in toxic behavior, such as drinking alcohol or smoking?
_____
_____
_____
_____

Name _____ Date _____

8. Are there any situations where you are modeling behavior for younger people? If so, where—and what behavior are you modeling?

_____

_____

_____

9. Name three healthy choices you made for yourself this week.

_____

_____

10. Name three adults who have helped in teaching you how to make healthy choices.

_____

_____

11. How would you interpret, "If you play, you pay."?

_____

_____

12. If you make your own decisions, you are responsible for your mind and your body. What does this mean?

_____

_____

_____

13. What can you do to avoid making toxic choices?

_____

_____

_____

14. Name three adults to whom you could go for help if you made a toxic choice that proved to be serious.

_____

_____

15. What can you do to make more healthy choices in your life?

_____

_____

CHAPTER 12
DO YOU KNOW WHERE YOU ARE GOING?

Have you ever played a game called, "Penny Hike"? It is an old game, but it is fun. You can play Penny Hike with a family member, a friend, your dog, or even by yourself. Here's what you do. You go to a street corner or road junction. You flip a penny. If it is heads, you go right. If it is tails, you go left. You walk along the street or road until you get to the next junction or intersection, where you flip the penny again.

A Penny Hike can take all day or much less. It is up to you. But, however long it takes, you can experience the sights, sounds, smells, and feel of not only embarking upon an adventure, but an adventure where you will go down new roads, some rough, some smooth. Some roads may be familiar to you and some may not.

There is a truth to this game of Penny Hike. The truth is that in this game, you never know where you are going or where you are going to end up or finish. Now, with hiking, that is okay, and frankly, that is much of the fun with Penny Hiking. However, some people take the same chances with their future careers as one would in a game of Penny Hike. Some people do not plan their careers; they simply come to a stopping point and make an uneducated guess about where to go next—much like flipping a coin.

In Penny Hiking, if you do not like where you end, you can, without a problem, start over or go back to the beginning. The downside or risk of not planning for a career is that a lifetime of "flipping the coin" does not easily allow for going back or starting over.

A young person who fails to make informed or intelligent career plans takes a big risk of a lifetime of discontent and wasted talent. Penny Hike decisions are made over the course of an afternoon or even a day. Career decisions are made over the course of a lifetime. With Penny Hiking it is not a big deal if you do not care for the spot where your journey ended. You can always start over another day. Not so with a career. If you do not like where you ended your career journey, it could take years of struggle, stress, and perhaps even much money to find your way back and then to start over. Unlike a Penny Hike, you can never go back to your career's point of origin. You just have to pick a place on your career path where you feel you may have become lost and start from there.

If the thought of ending up in the wrong career gives you a bit of anxiety, there is help for you. If you fear that you will not have a clue about what career path to choose, whether to go right or left, do not fear; there is help for you. And, if you are concerned that you may not know your own abilities and aptitudes, do not fear; there is help for you.

Where is this help? In middle school and high school, trained guidance counselors will be available for you to discuss your career goals or dreams. Your middle school and high school libraries will not only have books on choosing careers, but also on specific careers or professions. These two sources alone should help assist you as you progress through career development.

If you have not had the pleasure of meeting your guidance counselor or your school's career counselor, you need to make his or her acquaintance. It is never too soon for you, at this point as a middle school student, to begin exploring, reading about, and discussing careers. Your guidance counselor and your school, as well as your city or town's, librarian should be able to point you to information about careers, career development, and career choice.

At this point in your career development, you have the luxury of time—time to read about, think about, and explore any career imaginable. You can get on the Internet, watch videos, and talk to people about careers. You also have the luxury of time to participate in career testing. Find out from your guidance counselor which career tests may be available to you as a middle school student.

When you go into high school, visit your guidance counselor and check into career testing. Take the tests that are available to you and pay attention to the results of your tests. Career testing results are tools for you to use in career selection. You cannot learn too much too soon about yourself or careers. Arm yourself with career information steadily over time. You have a better chance of assimilating the information and using it.

Guidance counselors are your career advocates. Let them help you, but you must let them know that you want the help. Guidance counselors will guide you along your career development path and will give you more tools than just a coin, reducing your risk of ending up in a place where you did not care to go.

Guidance counselors, career tests, self-assessment, and helpful adults will assist you as you proceed through this most important part of your life—career development. From this point forward, you will be asked by well-meaning adults and relatives, "What do you want to be when you grow up?". Then you must ask yourself the same question. Things do not look ominous or threatening if you tell yourself that you make decisions one at a time, and one day at a time, and that there is always someone to turn to for help.

While you do have the rest of your life and you can be anything you want to be, taking the right steps to make a specific plan and choosing a specific career can be a stressful, frightening process if it is left undone until high school graduation. So you have to begin now, taking little steps, pacing yourself so you will not become frightened or discouraged.

At this point in your career development, you know that any research you have done on any career is a plus for you. Any self-assessment you have done is a plus for you. Any meetings with people who are in specific careers, who are willing to tell you about their careers, are a plus, as well. Knowing that you ultimately will have to make a career choice is good. You are aware that you, at some point, must decide in which direction you want to go.

You need to understand your choices, as well as your decisions, and the reasons for them. Knowing your options will help you make your decisions. For example, if you know that your family has been saving for your college education, you know that you have a college education waiting for you. If you know that you have made every effort to make good grades throughout middle school and high school, you know that you probably will be accepted by the college of your choice and perhaps there could be a chance for a scholarship.

You also know that you have more options than just college. You can get a job right after high school graduation if that is your choice. Maybe you can work after graduation and go to college part time, perhaps at night. When you make your choice about college or a job, make sure your decision is based upon sound and reasonable thinking. Do not make a decision without knowing the pros and the cons or the advantages and disadvantages.

There are other career steps one can take outside of college, too. There are training and technical schools that prepare students for careers such as hair styling, auto mechanics, drafting, plumbing, or electrical work.

Certification in a particular career might be obtained at a community or junior college, whereupon one could enter a career and continue an education at a four-year institution. One can earn an associate's degree after studying at a two-year junior college. There are two-year programs, for example, for paralegal and child-care attendants where one can earn a two-year certificate at a community college and be ready for employment.

Another option for high school graduates is the military. Today the military offers a high school graduate excellent training opportunities while in the military and money for college education after serving. When considering all options, remember that one can take college courses in the evening while working during the day. However, the military option is good only a certain number of years after high school graduation. One cannot decide after a certain age to go into the military. Check with your local military recruiter—the Army, Air Force, Navy, or Marines—if you think the military option might be for you.

This is a good time to remind you that the career development process, which requires you to make many decisions, can be challenging. However, if you find yourself struggling or having difficulty making decisions, help is not far away. A trusted adult is one of the safest and healthiest ways to help yourself. If you cannot think of an adult with whom you would like to talk, then perhaps you have a minister, a rabbi, a priest, or a Sunday School teacher with whom you can visit. And always remember that your school teacher and guidance counselor are good places to start when seeking help.

If you find a penny on a floor, save it for a Penny Hike, but do not use it as a tool in career guidance. For career guidance, turn to career testing, libraries, books, adult counselors, and self-assessment.

Career Search	CHAPTER 12: Do You Know Where You are Going?

Name _____ Date _____

WHAT DO YOU THINK?

1. What are some of the ways you can research a career?
_____
_____
_____

2. What is a guidance counselor? Who is your school's guidance counselor?
_____
_____

3. How do you feel about talking to your guidance counselor about careers?
_____
_____

4. What are some of the options, other than college, open to you after high school graduation?
_____
_____
_____

5. What would be one of the advantages of entering the military after high school?
_____
_____

6. Who, besides your guidance counselor, could you visit with about your career concerns?
_____
_____
_____

7. How many sources can you list for career guidance assistance?
_____
_____
_____
_____

CHAPTER 13
INCREASING YOUR CHANCES FOR SUCCESS

Someone once said, when asked if they believed in luck, "Luck? Oh, sure. I believe in luck. And I have discovered that the harder I work, the more I have of it."

When you watch ice skaters, pianists, actors, or singers perform, you might be tempted to think that their talent is a result of luck. Some people who allow themselves to think that luck is a mysterious power beyond their control end up as failures. They convince themselves that luck is something like rain that falls on successful people, but does not fall on themselves. So, they quit or give up, turning their backs on their own inherent talents, leaving them to sputter and die.

When you see an Olympic athlete perform incredible physical feats, you might think how lucky that athlete is to be in the Olympics. But, you do not see how many hours, weeks, months, and years that athlete spent in practice, developing his or her ability. When you hear a singer, you might think how lucky he or she is to lead such a glamorous life, but you do not see how much effort, how many years of practice went into training the voice that you are hearing.

Middle schoolers, pay attention here. **LUCK IS WHAT HAPPENS WHEN OPPORTUNITY AND PREPARATION MEET.** In other words, if you are prepared when the opportunity comes along, your chances for "luck" are great. An Olympic athlete can win a medal only with work and practice (preparation) before the Olympics (opportunity).

One's talents or aptitudes may be fortuitously bestowed by a spin of the genetic wheel, but it is only by effort and hard work that talent will fully develop. You are born with a natural ability to do something unique, but it is only through your pursuit of knowledge, practice, and hard work that your talent will develop to its full extent.

Beethoven spent hours, days, and years writing and practicing his music. Thomas Edison constantly experimented with any materials he could find. Einstein had a curiosity about math, and Maria Tallchief perfected her dance over many years.

It is said that there once was a woman who, after attending the piano concert of a famous pianist, went backstage to meet the pianist. "I would give anything to play like you do," gushed the woman to the pianist. The pianist responded, "No, I don't think you would. You see, I've given my life to it."

Talents will lie still and dormant—undeveloped—if no effort is made to develop them. Zig Ziglar, a famous motivational speaker and author of many books, once stated, "I've read where women have given birth to boys and girls, but thus far, I have never read where a woman has given birth to a salesman, or a doctor, lawyer, artist, engineer, etc. By choice and training, not by birth, they become what they wish to become." Mr. Ziglar points out clearly that choosing to work and train your talent is the key to success.

What choice will you make? How hard will you work or train to become what it is you wish to become?

With in-depth knowledge of yourself and extensive, in-depth knowledge about careers, you will ease into career choice. Because the ultimate choice of a career should be a process developed over a lengthy period of time, the process is referred to as **career development**.

Your developing knowledge and understanding about yourself and careers is referred to as **career maturity**. The information and exercises throughout this book are to encourage your career development and move you along to career maturity.

As a middle school student, you have plenty of time and opportunity to gather and assimilate career information. There are fun, creative ways to learn more about careers and about yourself. If you begin while in middle school, you will have an advantage when difficult, career-path decisions come your way.

Listed below are ideas from which you can choose to help increase your chances for career success:

1. **School Career Fairs.** Volunteer when it is time for your school's career fair. There is always a need for posters, distribution of announcements, and help with registration, setting up, and so on. If your school does not host a career fair, offer to help organize one. Even elementary schools have them, so why not your middle school? Volunteer to seek speakers. It is an excellent way to get better acquainted with adults who are employed or are retired from various careers, ranging from accounting to zoo keeping.

2. **Other Career Fairs.** If possible, attend career fairs in your community. Small towns organize them to help businesses and students. High schools, junior or community colleges, and local colleges and universities will host career fairs. Seek permission to visit a career fair and go. This is an opportunity to hear a number of people representing various careers talk about their present or past careers.

3. **Career Retirees.** Visit with older adults who have retired from their careers. Chances are that they will not have a tight schedule at this stage in their lives and they, most likely, would be delighted to visit with you about their past work. This resource is valuable, but few people take advantage of it. Be one of the few.

4. **On-Site Career Visits.** Visiting someone on the job is an excellent way to determine your interest in a particular career. If veterinary medicine, nursing, piano tuning, or auto technology are careers that interest you, check with your parents or teachers about arranging on-site visits with various career individuals. Spend a morning with the director of your local zoo, spend an afternoon with a minister, walk the store aisles with a store manager, attend a class taught by a college professor, get permission to visit a police chief, and observe judges, court clerks, paralegals, and attorneys in a court room. On-site career visits will add depth to your career knowledge.

5. **Begin a Career File.** Add any and all information about careers from newspapers, magazines, and professional journals. Peruse your career file frequently, and keep your information up to date.

6. **Begin a Career Scrapbook.** This is fun, and your creativity can soar. All your cut-and-paste desires will be met as you pore through periodicals, post cards, and old greeting

cards, pasting in those poems, clippings, and pictures representing anything and everything, from interior design to mountain climbing. Seeing your interests displayed in a scrapbook will teach you about your career leanings.

7. **Begin a Career Journal.** Enter frequently your thoughts and feelings about careers as you experience them. Writing or maintaining a journal has often been used as a way to gain true insight. You might detect, over time, a career thought pattern.

8. **Do Good Deeds.** Every time you do a good deed, whether it be filling water glasses at the local nursing home or babysitting for free, you learn something about yourself. Try it. You will accept yourself more and treat yourself better. This will, in turn, encourage you to be attentive and receptive to ways you can be nicer to yourself. Your self-concept will rise, and you will be a step closer to career maturity.

9. **Keep Letters of Reference.** Ask relatives, friends, teachers, your clergy, and neighbors to write letters of reference for you, even though you are not applying for a job. It is a good exercise in learning how to gather this type of information when it is needed. After studying the letters, you most certainly will learn how others view you. File the letters in your personal file.

10. **Read Biographies.** Reading about successful people is informative and fun. You will discover that even successful people had to find their way, just like you. Visit your library. Read about people who took the time to tell their story. You will discover that many successful people never thought that they would find themselves in their chosen career, while others knew their career direction from the start.

Career development can be complicated. It can be, but it doesn't have to be. Keep in mind that it is not a one-time event, but a long-term process and can, at times, be a difficult process to handle alone. Remember that career awareness leads to career development, which leads to career maturity. There are resources all around you, and there are a number of adults who can help you. These adults are teachers, counselors, clergy members, neighbors, parents, and caregivers. Ask them for help. It is the strong and the wise student who asks for help, gets help, and then uses that help.

Do not allow yourself to get discouraged if answers to your career questions seem difficult to find. While you are seeking the ideal career, you are experiencing and observing, learning various developmental skills that will bridge your way to the next task.

Even if you sometimes feel that you are making no progress related to careers, remember that you are continually building and developing basic skills such as communication—verbal, visual, and written—computing, and social skills. These are essentials, not only in a career, but in life. Without having mastered the basics, a career would offer you little more than stress and frustration.

Career Search   CHAPTER 13: Increasing Your Chances for Success

Name _____ Date _____

WHAT DO YOU THINK?

1. Do you consider yourself to be lucky? Explain why or why not.

_____

_____

2. List three healthy choices you have made in the last year that could influence your future career choices.

_____

_____

3. List three careers that you are certain you do not care to pursue. Then explain, for each, why.

_____

_____

_____

4. On your own paper, write a letter of reference for yourself as you would like it to read 10 to 15 years from now.

5. What things have you already done that you could put in a career scrapbook or journal?

_____

_____

_____

6. On your own paper, write a letter of reference or recommendation for an adult you admire.

7. List three people, living or dead, whom you admire. Now describe what talents or traits you have that each of the people you have chosen also possess.

_____

_____

_____

_____

Name _____ Date _____

8. Have you won an award? Did you complete a huge, long-term project, such as a science fair project, or have you built or created something at home? Name three accomplishments of which you are very, very proud. Then, write down three talents or traits that helped you achieve your accomplishments.

_____

_____

_____

_____

9. List three careers that would allow you to use the talents you used to achieve your accomplishments.

_____

_____

10. Write down three things you think make you different from anyone else. What do you think are the problems of having these differences?

_____

_____

_____

11. What do you think are the advantages of those things that make you different from others?

_____

_____

12. Can you think of anything that might get in the way of you being successful in school? List three things that could keep you from working hard, studying, and making good grades.

_____

_____

13. What can you do to make sure those things you listed in number 12 do not get in the way of you being a successful student?

_____

_____

_____

CHAPTER 14
CLASSROOM ACTIVITIES

1. **Plan a Super, Self-Concept Session.** One person, referred to as the "guest," sits in the middle of the room in the "neat seat." Taking turns, each student tells something positive about the "guest." Appoint someone as the recorder who writes down all the comments. When everyone has commented, the recorder gives the list of positive comments to the "guest." Everyone should have a turn as "guest," and everyone should participate in making positive comments. This creates community, peer support, and encourages positive self-concepts.

2. **Have Students Present Reports on Various Careers,** complete with visual aids. Allow the student to select a particular career of their interest, do the research, and present the information.

3. **Create a Classroom Career Bulletin Board.** Allow students who are reporting on careers to post career information that is relative to the reports.

4. **Have Students Keep a Career Notebook** in which they maintain information about themselves regarding their strengths and weaknesses, likes and dislikes, positive characteristics, abilities and aptitudes, and interests. Have them add information about the careers in which they are interested. Award certificates for informative, neat, and organized notebooks.

5. **Make a Game Out of Guessing Careers.** After a career is described, guess what it is. See the *Dictionary of Occupational Titles,* the *Guide for Occupational Exploration,* or *Careers and You* or the *Careers* series from Mark Twain Media, Inc., for career descriptions.

6. **Encourage Self-Awareness Among Students** by asking students to make a list of their own positive attributes, talents, skills, traits, and characteristics. Then ask them to write themselves a letter of recommendation for a hypothetical job.

7. **Encourage Awareness of the Talent in Others** by asking students to list the names of everyone in the class. Next to each name, write a career title that the students think would match the student.

8. **Spend Some Class Time on Values and How They are Needed,** particularly on the job. Encourage discussion about respect, ethics, honesty, trust, and how these values relate to careers.

9. **Invite Guest Speakers** from your community to speak about values. Select speakers who might, to the students, represent a particular value. For example, a police officer might represent honesty, a judge might represent fairness, an athlete could speak about good sportsmanship, as well as respect and trust. A minister could address values in

general. Ask students to take and keep notes of guest speakers' comments in their career notebooks.

10. **Practice Interview Skills.** It is never too early to teach students about presenting themselves to employers. Set up role-playing exercises so students can practice how to prepare for and handle an interview. Have the students pair off and play the role of interviewer and interviewee. Then reverse roles. The exercise can be made more realistic by having each student prepare a resume to submit to the interview.

11. **Have Students Peruse a Sunday Newspaper.** Ask that they cut out four or five ads for job openings, taping them to a sheet of paper. On the paper, have them write why the job ad appealed to them and what they would need to do in the future in order to qualify for the job.

12. **Arrange to Get Students Onto College Campuses** and see that they walk through the career counseling office. Plan to spend time on campus sitting in on various classes and touring the campus. This is an effective way to convey to students that college and careers are part of their future.

13. **Invite a Guidance Counselor** from a high school or college to visit the class and invite him or her to speak about career planning and development.

14. **Invite a City or State Government Official** to visit the class and describe the world of work in the public sector.

15. **Make a Positive-Image Board.** Over the period of one semester, have students write down one positive, descriptive word about themselves each day. Write each word on a small slip of paper and drop it, daily, into a small box. At the end of the semester, the student is to paste their picture in the middle of a piece of cardboard and paste the positive words around the picture. Have a "positive image board day" to display all the posters.

16. **Have Each Student Interview Three People in Different Careers.** Have them write the interviews as reports and present them to the class.

17. **Have Each Student Read Three Books About Careers** and present at least one book report to the class.

18. **Brainstorm in Class With a "Career Alphabet."** Starting with the letter "A," list as many careers as the students can recall that begin with each letter of the alphabet.

19. **Frequently Delve Into Unique or Unusual Careers.** Encourage research into unique or unusual careers by presenting information about unique careers that are not always considered. Present videos, guess-the-career challenges, and invite guest speakers to talk about unusual careers. This will give students a broad base of career information and choices.

CHAPTER 15
TIPS FOR THE TEACHER

1. **Career Education is an Integral Part of Teaching.** Students perform better with a good self-concept. We know that a child's academic ability has a direct effect on the child's self-concept and self-esteem. The self-concept has a direct effect on the child's career maturity. Education continues to be a cornerstone of positive career development. Teachers' contributions to healthy, positive career development is invaluable.

2. **Students' Efforts to Enhance Self-Concept and Self-Esteem Should be Encouraged and Recognized.** Exercises that encourage the student to master a particular task are ideal for enhancing the self-concept. Positive recognition of mastering the task can be accomplished in many ways such as stickers, tokens, name display, or even applause.

3. **Be Sensitive to Those Students Who are Unfamiliar With Careers.** Students who have not been exposed to many career options may demonstrate lack of interest in a career when it may be that the student is simply not familiar with that career.

4. **Provide Career Exploration Opportunities Through Speakers,** both male and female, representing a variety of careers, from a variety of cultures. This encourages and sparks interest in both the student who has had a wide exposure to careers and the student who is very unfamiliar with careers. Enlist the support and assistance of community and business leaders.

5. **Be Sensitive to Those Children Who Appear Apathetic,** who do not understand or know their capability for success. By helping these children see their positive aptitudes, abilities, and traits, their chances for career success are greatly increased.

6. **Be Sensitive to Career Development Strategies for Various Cultures.** Generally, students are taught assertiveness, particularly regarding the job search and interviews. However, children from some cultures are taught to be silent until addressed. A bowed head and lowered eyes are signs of respect for their elders. Be careful not to misinterpret the manner of children from different cultural backgrounds.

7. **Be Sensitive to Career Development Strategies for the Handicapped or Special Needs Student.** A wealth of information is available regarding career guidance for the handicapped, particularly through state rehabilitation agencies. Efforts to strengthen peer relationships and self-concept will benefit not only the special-needs student, but all students.

8. **Allow Time for Discussion of Values With Students.** Point out the role values play in career choice. Invite a business or community leader to visit the classroom and talk about the role that values have played in his or her career.

9. **In Career Development, It is Important That Short-Term Goals Relate to Long-Term Goals.** Encourage goal setting both in and out of the classroom. Have students set one or two short-term goals per week, one goal per month, one goal per semester, and one goal per school year. Recognize and honor those students who set and achieve worthwhile goals.

10. **It is Important That Students are Consistently Exposed to Career Development.** Conveying the relationship of ongoing activity with future careers and career success helps the student see the potential brought about by present effort. Career bulletin boards are a positive and helpful method of illustrating various career options. Career notebooks are creative and fun methods of honoring the students' career interests. Assigning "cut-and-paste" tasks may sound elementary, but this type of task allows the students a visual method of enjoying and organizing their innermost thoughts about career exploration.

11. **It is Important That Students Understand the Importance of Good Study Habits** early in their education. While students are constantly reminded that good grades count, sometimes the goal of a good grade appears too far out of reach, or the student views a good grade as lackluster in comparison to instant gratification. If time permits or if an opportunity arises, spend time focusing on regular, consistent, study habits and the benefits of good study habits. Perhaps some relaxation exercises during class and pointing out the reduced stress that comes with the practice of regular study habits would encourage regular study without focusing so much on "good grades." Remind the students that good grades are just one of the rewards of healthy study habits.

12. **Convey to Students That Healthy Study Habits are Comparable to a Savings Account.** Note that "good grades" are one of the rewards of regular study, like a future purchase is a reward of a savings account. Indicate to students that by investing in their study account, one can reap investment rewards of good grades, which will allow for a major "purchase" or "reward," such as a college scholarship or acceptance into the college of their choice. Consider creating a "passbook" of study habit hours. After a semester of recorded study hours, compare the hours to the resulting grades. Consider offering an interest reward—perhaps certificates from local merchants or tokens for special school privileges, such as being first in lunch line, and so forth.

13. **Encourage the Students to Invest in Themselves.** Perhaps at the beginning of the school year, allow the students to create a portfolio that, at the end of the school year, the students can put on display. Instruct the students to create sections in their notebooks that will show how they have spent their time in the school year as a part of the community, as a part of school organizations, and as a part of the class. Show them how to exhibit their involvement in their lives as students, children, group participants, community members, and so on. At the end of the year, students will see their own productivity in a notebook that will give each of them a sense of accomplishment and pride.

14. **Encourage Positive Futures** by instructing each student to write a play, script, or story about their lives and to project into the future about their lives as adults. Once written, discuss the stories with the students. For those with positive plans, question them on what they can do to ensure that outcome. For those students with less-than-positive plans, question them on how they can change their future so it will be a positive one.

15. **Try to Be Sensitive to Those Students Who Have Unusual or Difficult Circumstances.** Not all students have ideal conditions in which to develop. While many students receive healthy encouragement, there are some students who do well to survive the day. Keep in mind that you, unknowingly, may be the only positive influence in a child's life. Taking steps to reduce your own stress, to be good to yourself, and to take care of yourself, will allow you to be a better, happier role model for children who will grow up to be our leaders of tomorrow. Be kind to yourself. You never know who will need your extra strength.

Career Search WHAT DO YOU THINK?: Self-Assessment

Name _____ Date _____

WHAT DO YOU THINK?
SELF-ASSESSMENT

On a scale of 1 to 10, with 10 being the highest, rate yourself on the following. Circle the appropriate number for each talent/trait.

a. friendly	1	2	3	4	5	6	7	8	9	10
b. considerate to others	1	2	3	4	5	6	7	8	9	10
c. dependable	1	2	3	4	5	6	7	8	9	10
d. artistic	1	2	3	4	5	6	7	8	9	10
e. quiet	1	2	3	4	5	6	7	8	9	10
f. talented	1	2	3	4	5	6	7	8	9	10
g. problem solving	1	2	3	4	5	6	7	8	9	10
h. efficient	1	2	3	4	5	6	7	8	9	10
i. helping others	1	2	3	4	5	6	7	8	9	10
j. working with numbers	1	2	3	4	5	6	7	8	9	10
k. imaginative	1	2	3	4	5	6	7	8	9	10
l. musical	1	2	3	4	5	6	7	8	9	10
m. practical	1	2	3	4	5	6	7	8	9	10
n. persistent	1	2	3	4	5	6	7	8	9	10
o. orderly	1	2	3	4	5	6	7	8	9	10
p. convincing	1	2	3	4	5	6	7	8	9	10
q. kind	1	2	3	4	5	6	7	8	9	10
r. cooperative	1	2	3	4	5	6	7	8	9	10
s. expressive	1	2	3	4	5	6	7	8	9	10
t. conservative	1	2	3	4	5	6	7	8	9	10
u. ambitious	1	2	3	4	5	6	7	8	9	10
v. energetic	1	2	3	4	5	6	7	8	9	10
w. curious	1	2	3	4	5	6	7	8	9	10
x. self-confident	1	2	3	4	5	6	7	8	9	10
y. analytical	1	2	3	4	5	6	7	8	9	10
z. enjoy the outdoors	1	2	3	4	5	6	7	8	9	10

© Mark Twain Media, Inc., Publishers

Career Search   WHAT DO YOU THINK?: Self-Assessment

Name _____ Date _____

Write down those talents/traits that you scored yourself with a 6 or above.

Talents/Traits: _____

_____

_____

_____

_____

_____

_____

From this self-evaluation, what careers do you think best suit a person with your talents/traits?

_____

_____

_____

_____

_____

_____

_____

_____

_____

_____

_____

_____

JUST BECAUSE OF YOU

The more you learn today,
the more you will know and want to learn.
The more you know,
The more you will understand yourself
and the world.
The more you understand yourself and the world,
the better career choices you will make.
The better career choices that you make,
the happier you will be in life.
The happier you are,
the better friend, family member, and citizen you will be.
The better person you are,
the more satisfied and successful you will be.
The more personally satisfied and successful you are,
the healthier you will be.
The healthier you are,
the longer you will live.
The longer you live,
the more you can enjoy life.
The more you enjoy life,
the more people will want to be around you.
The more people are around you,
the more they will want to know your secret
to a long and happy life.
The more people want to know your secret
for a long and happy life,
the more you can teach others
how to be a success.
The more you teach others
how to be a success,
the more the world will benefit . . .
just because of you.

Sherry Strong

BIBLIOGRAPHY

Careers in Business Operations. (1997). Mark Twain Media/Carson-Dellosa Publishing Company, Inc.

Careers in Sales, Marketing, and Management. (1997). Mark Twain Media/Carson-Dellosa Publishing Company, Inc.

Careers in Science. (1997). Mark Twain Media/Carson-Dellosa Publishing Company, Inc.

Careers in the Arts. (1997). Mark Twain Media/Carson-Dellosa Publishing Company, Inc.

Careers in the Social Services. (1997). Mark Twain Media/Carson-Dellosa Publishing Company, Inc.

Careers in the Technical Fields. (1997). Mark Twain Media/Carson-Dellosa Publishing Company, Inc.

Havighurst, R. (1981). *Developmental Tasks and Education* (3rd ed.). New York: Longman.

Kapes, Jerome T. and Mastie, Majorie Moran (Eds.) (1988). *A Counselor's Guide to Career Assessment Instruments* (2nd ed.). Alexandria, Virginia: The National Career Development Association.

Kaplan, Paul S. (1990). *Educational Psychology for Tomorrow's Teacher.* St. Paul, MN: West Publishing Company.

Lueckenhoff, Linda (1993). *Careers and You.* Mark Twain Media/Carson-Dellosa Publishing Company, Inc.

McWilliams, John-Roger & Peter (1992). *Wealth 101.* Prelude Press, Inc.

Singer, Sam and Hilgard, Henry R. (1978). *The Biology of People.* San Francisco: W. H. Freeman and Company.

Trembly, Dean (1974). *Learning to Use Your Aptitudes.* San Luis Obispo, CA: Erin Hills Publishers.

Willerman, Lee and Cohen, David B. (1990). *Psychopathology.* McGraw-Hill Publishing Company.

Wilson, David W. and Wilson, Ruth A. (1997). *Promoting Positive Values for School and Everyday Life.* Mark Twain Media/Carson-Dellosa Publishing Company, Inc.

Ziglar, Zig (1977). *See You at the Top.* Pelican Publishing Company, Inc.

Zunker, Vernon G. (1990). *Career Counseling Applied Concepts of Life Planning.* Pacific Grove, CA: Brooks/Cole Publishing Company.